Renal Diet Cookbook for Beginners UK

150 Budget-Friendly, Nutrient-Rich, and Tasty Renal Recipes

Table of contents

Breakfast Delights

Breakfast Quinoa with Blueberries

Yield: 4 servings | Prep time: 5 minutes | Cook time: 15 minutes

Ingredients:

- 150g quinoa, rinsed and drained
- 475ml water
- 100g fresh blueberries
- 30g chopped walnuts
- 1 teaspoon cinnamon
- 1 tablespoon honey
- 125ml almond milk (unsweetened)

Directions:

1. In a medium saucepan, bring the water to a boil. Add quinoa and reduce heat to low. Cover and simmer for 12-15 minutes, or until quinoa is cooked and water is absorbed.
2. Remove the saucepan from heat, fluff the quinoa with a fork, and let it cool for a few minutes.
3. Stir in the cinnamon and honey. Divide the quinoa into bowls.
4. Top each bowl with blueberries and walnuts. Pour almond milk over the top.

Nutritional Information: Per serving: 200 calories, 6g protein, 30g carbohydrates, 6g fat, 4g fiber, 0mg cholesterol, 10mg sodium, 170mg potassium.

Berry and Yogurt Parfait

Yield: 4 servings | Prep time: 10 minutes | Cook time: 0 minutes

Ingredients:

- 400g Greek yogurt (low-fat, unsweetened)
- 200g mixed berries (blueberries, raspberries, strawberries)
- 40g granola (low-sodium, no added sugar)
- 2 tablespoons honey
- 1 teaspoon vanilla extract

Directions:

1. Wash the mixed berries thoroughly and set aside.
2. In a small bowl, mix the Greek yogurt with honey and vanilla extract until well combined.
3. In four glasses or bowls, layer the ingredients: Start with a layer of Greek yogurt, then add a layer of berries, and sprinkle granola on top.
4. Repeat the layers, finishing with a layer of berries on top.
5. Chill in the refrigerator for 15 minutes before serving, if desired.

Nutritional Information: Per serving: 150 calories, 8g protein, 24g carbohydrates, 2g fat, 3g fiber, 5mg cholesterol, 45mg sodium, 150mg potassium.

Almond and Banana Smoothie

Yield: 2 servings | Prep time: 5 minutes | Cook time: 0 minutes

Ingredients:

- 1 large banana, sliced
- 240ml almond milk (unsweetened)
- 1 tablespoon almond butter
- 1 tablespoon honey
- 1/2 teaspoon vanilla extract
- A pinch of ground cinnamon

Directions:

1. Place all the ingredients in a blender and blend until smooth.
2. Taste and adjust sweetness, if necessary.
3. Pour the smoothie into two glasses and serve immediately.

Nutritional Information: Per serving: 135 calories, 2g protein, 24g carbohydrates, 4g fat, 2g fiber, 0mg cholesterol, 90mg sodium, 225mg potassium.

Savory Breakfast Rice Bowl

Yield: 4 servings | Prep time: 10 minutes | Cook time: 20 minutes

Ingredients:

- 200g uncooked long-grain white rice
- 500ml water
- 1 tbsp olive oil
- 1 small onion, diced
- 2 cloves garlic, minced
- 150g mushrooms, sliced
- 100g spinach leaves, washed and roughly chopped
- Salt and pepper to taste
- 4 large eggs
- Optional toppings: chopped herbs, grated cheese, hot sauce

Directions:

1. In a medium-sized saucepan, bring the water to a boil. Add the rice and a pinch of salt, reduce the heat to low, cover, and simmer for 15-20 minutes, or until the rice is cooked through.
2. While the rice is cooking, heat the olive oil in a large skillet over medium heat. Add the diced onion and cook for 3-4 minutes, or until it becomes translucent.
3. Add the garlic and mushrooms to the skillet, and cook for another 5 minutes, or until the mushrooms are soft.
4. Stir in the chopped spinach, and cook for 2 minutes, or until the spinach is wilted. Season with salt and pepper to taste.
5. In a separate non-stick skillet, fry the eggs to your desired level of doneness.
6. To assemble the bowls, divide the cooked rice among four bowls. Top each bowl with the sautéed vegetables and a fried egg. Add any optional toppings, if desired.

Nutritional Information: Per serving: 270 calories, 9g protein, 42g carbohydrates, 7g fat, 2g fiber, 185mg cholesterol, 150mg sodium, 250mg potassium.

Low-Potassium Oat Pancakes

Yield: 4 servings (2 pancakes each) | Prep time: 10 minutes | Cook time: 15 minutes

Ingredients:

- 100g oats, ground into flour
- 1 teaspoon baking powder (low-sodium)
- 1/2 teaspoon baking soda
- 1/2 teaspoon ground cinnamon
- 1 tablespoon sugar
- 120ml milk (low-fat)
- 1 large egg
- 1 teaspoon vanilla extract
- Cooking spray or oil for frying
- 120ml fresh berries for topping (optional)
- 2 tablespoons maple syrup for drizzling (optional)

Directions:

1. In a large bowl, combine the ground oats, baking powder, baking soda, cinnamon, and sugar.
2. In a separate bowl, whisk together the milk, egg, and vanilla extract.
3. Pour the wet ingredients into the dry ingredients and stir until just combined. The batter will be thick.
4. Heat a non-stick skillet over medium heat and lightly coat with cooking spray or oil.
5. Pour 1/4 cup of the batter into the skillet and spread it into a circle. Cook until bubbles form on the surface, about 2 minutes. Flip and cook the other side for an additional 2 minutes, or until golden brown.
6. Repeat with the remaining batter, making a total of 8 pancakes.
7. Serve hot, topped with fresh berries and a drizzle of maple syrup, if desired.

Nutritional Information: Per serving (2 pancakes): 150 calories, 5g protein, 25g carbohydrates, 3g fat, 2g fiber, 40mg cholesterol, 150mg sodium, 150mg potassium.

Overnight Chia Seed Pudding

Yield: 4 servings | Prep time: 5 minutes | Cook time: 0 minutes (refrigerate overnight)

Ingredients:

- 60g chia seeds
- 500ml unsweetened almond milk
- 1 tsp vanilla extract
- 2 tbsp honey or maple syrup (adjust to taste)
- Fresh berries for topping (optional)
- Sliced almonds for topping (optional)

Directions:

1. In a mixing bowl, combine the chia seeds, almond milk, vanilla extract, and honey or maple syrup. Stir well to ensure that the chia seeds are evenly distributed.
2. Cover the bowl with plastic wrap or a lid and refrigerate for at least 4 hours, or preferably overnight. The chia seeds will absorb the liquid and create a thick pudding-like texture.
3. Before serving, give the pudding a good stir to break up any clumps. Divide the pudding into individual servings and top with fresh berries and sliced almonds if desired.

Nutritional Information: Per serving: 140 calories, 5g protein, 16g carbohydrates, 7g fat, 9g fiber, 0mg cholesterol, 75mg sodium, 150mg potassium.

Scrambled Tofu and Veggies

Yield: 4 servings | Prep time: 10 minutes | Cook time: 10 minutes

Ingredients:

- 400g firm tofu, crumbled
- 1 tablespoon olive oil
- 1 small onion, finely chopped (about 75g)
- 1 medium red bell pepper, diced (about 100g)
- 100g mushrooms, sliced
- 1 teaspoon turmeric
- 1 teaspoon paprika
- Salt and pepper to taste
- 2 tablespoons fresh parsley, chopped

Directions:

1. In a large non-stick skillet, heat the olive oil over medium heat. Add the onion, bell pepper, and mushrooms. Cook until the vegetables are soft, about 5 minutes.
2. Add the crumbled tofu, turmeric, and paprika. Season with salt and pepper. Cook for another 5 minutes, stirring occasionally.
3. Remove from heat and stir in the chopped parsley.
4. Serve hot, as a filling for a sandwich, wrap, or on its own with a side salad.

Nutritional Information: Per serving: 140 calories, 12g protein, 10g carbohydrates, 7g fat, 3g fiber, 0mg cholesterol, 15mg sodium, 310mg potassium.

Polenta Breakfast Bowl with Veggies

Yield: 4 servings | Prep time: 10 minutes | Cook time: 30 minutes

Ingredients:

- 120g polenta
- 750ml water
- 1/2 tsp salt
- 2 tbsp olive oil
- 1 small onion, chopped
- 1 bell pepper, chopped
- 100g mushrooms, sliced
- 100g cherry tomatoes, halved
- 50g spinach, chopped
- 2 cloves garlic, minced
- 1/4 tsp black pepper
- Fresh herbs (basil, parsley, or thyme) for garnish

Directions:

1. In a medium-sized saucepan, bring water and salt to a boil. Gradually whisk in the polenta, stirring constantly. Reduce heat to low and simmer, stirring frequently, until polenta is thick and creamy, about 25-30 minutes. Remove from heat.
2. While the polenta is cooking, heat olive oil in a large skillet over medium heat. Add onions and bell peppers, and sauté until softened, about 5 minutes.
3. Add mushrooms and garlic to the skillet, and sauté for another 3 minutes.
4. Add cherry tomatoes and spinach, and sauté until spinach is wilted and tomatoes are heated through, about 2 minutes. Season with black pepper.
5. Serve the polenta in bowls, topped with the sautéed vegetables. Garnish with fresh herbs of your choice.

Nutritional Information: Per serving: 180 calories, 4g protein, 29g carbohydrates, 6g fat, 4g fiber, 0mg cholesterol, 300mg sodium, 250mg potassium.

Muesli with Fresh Berries

Yield: 4 servings | Prep time: 5 minutes | Cook time: 0 minutes

Ingredients:

- 150g rolled oats (low-sodium)
- 30g chopped almonds
- 30g dried apricots, chopped
- 240ml almond milk (unsweetened)
- 200g mixed berries (strawberries, blueberries, raspberries)
- 2 tablespoons honey or maple syrup

Directions:

1. In a large mixing bowl, combine the rolled oats, chopped almonds, and chopped apricots.
2. Divide the mixture into four bowls.
3. Top each bowl with almond milk and mixed berries.
4. Drizzle each serving with honey or maple syrup, as desired.
5. Serve immediately.

Nutritional Information: Per serving: 220 calories, 6g protein, 36g carbohydrates, 6g fat, 5g fiber, 0mg cholesterol, 15mg sodium, 120mg potassium.

Spiced Porridge with Raisins

Yield: 4 servings | Prep time: 5 minutes | Cook time: 10 minutes

Ingredients:

- 150g porridge oats
- 720ml water
- 1/2 teaspoon ground cinnamon
- 1/4 teaspoon ground nutmeg
- 1/4 teaspoon ground ginger
- 50g raisins
- 2 tablespoons brown sugar or honey
- 240ml milk (low-fat)

Directions:

1. In a saucepan, combine the porridge oats, water, cinnamon, nutmeg, and ginger.
2. Bring the mixture to a simmer over medium heat, stirring occasionally.
3. Reduce the heat to low and continue to cook, stirring occasionally, until the porridge thickens, about 5-7 minutes.
4. Stir in the raisins and brown sugar or honey.
5. Divide the porridge among four bowls, and serve with a splash of milk on top.

Nutritional Information: Per serving: 210 calories, 7g protein, 40g carbohydrates, 3g fat, 4g fiber, 5mg cholesterol, 60mg sodium, 220mg potassium.

Creamy Berry Smoothie Bowl

Yield: 2 servings | Prep time: 10 minutes | Cook time: 0 minutes

Ingredients:

- 150g mixed berries (strawberries, blueberries, raspberries), fresh or frozen
- 1 ripe banana
- 120ml almond milk
- 120g Greek yogurt (low-fat)
- 2 tsp honey
- 2 tbsp granola
- 2 tbsp shredded coconut
- Fresh berries and mint leaves for garnish

Directions:

1. In a blender, combine the mixed berries, banana, almond milk, Greek yogurt, and honey. Blend until smooth and creamy.
2. Pour the smoothie into two bowls.
3. Top each bowl with granola and shredded coconut.
4. Garnish with fresh berries and mint leaves.
5. Serve immediately and enjoy!

Nutritional Information: Per serving: 220 calories, 8g protein, 35g carbohydrates, 6g fat, 5g fiber, 5mg cholesterol, 60mg sodium, 350mg potassium.

Toasted Whole Grain Bread with Avocado

Yield: 2 servings | Prep time: 5 minutes | Cook time: 2 minutes

Ingredients:

- 4 slices whole grain bread
- 1 ripe avocado
- 1/2 lemon, juiced
- Salt and pepper to taste
- Optional toppings: sliced radishes, chopped tomatoes, fresh herbs

Directions:

1. Toast the slices of whole grain bread until they are crispy and golden-brown.
2. While the bread is toasting, cut the avocado in half and remove the pit. Scoop the flesh into a bowl and mash it with a fork.
3. Add the lemon juice, salt, and pepper to the mashed avocado and mix well.
4. Spread the mashed avocado mixture onto the toasted bread slices.
5. Top with any optional toppings if desired and serve.

Nutritional Information: Per serving: 230 calories, 7g protein, 27g carbohydrates, 12g fat, 9g fiber, 0mg cholesterol, 160mg sodium, 540mg potassium.

Spinach and Mushroom Omelette

Yield: 2 servings | Prep time: 10 minutes | Cook time: 10 minutes

Ingredients:

- 4 large eggs
- 60ml milk (low-fat)
- Salt and pepper to taste
- 1 tablespoon olive oil
- 1 small onion, chopped (about 75g)
- 100g mushrooms, sliced
- 100g fresh spinach leaves
- 50g grated cheddar cheese (optional)

Directions:

1. In a bowl, whisk together the eggs, milk, salt, and pepper until well combined. Set aside.
2. In a non-stick skillet, heat the olive oil over medium heat. Add the onion and mushrooms, and cook until the vegetables are soft, about 5 minutes.
3. Add the spinach to the skillet and cook until wilted, about 2 minutes.
4. Pour the egg mixture over the vegetables in the skillet and cook without stirring until the edges of the omelette are set, about 2-3 minutes.
5. Sprinkle the cheese over half of the omelette, if using, and fold the omelette in half. Cook for another 2 minutes until the cheese is melted and the omelette is fully set.
6. Slide the omelette onto a plate, cut in half, and serve.

Nutritional Information: Per serving: 220 calories, 16g protein, 8g carbohydrates, 14g fat, 2g fiber, 370mg cholesterol, 220mg sodium, 460mg potassium.

Berry Breakfast Muffins

Yield: 12 servings (12 muffins) | Prep time: 15 minutes | Cook time: 25 minutes

Ingredients:

- 200g all-purpose flour
- 100g whole wheat flour
- 150g granulated sugar
- 2 tsp baking powder
- 1/2 tsp baking soda
- 1/4 tsp salt
- 2 large eggs
- 120ml vegetable oil
- 200ml milk (low-fat)
- 1 tsp vanilla extract
- 200g mixed berries (blueberries, raspberries, strawberries, etc.)

Directions:

1. Preheat your oven to 180°C (350°F). Line a muffin tin with paper muffin cups or lightly grease the cups.
2. In a large bowl, combine the all-purpose flour, whole wheat flour, granulated sugar, baking powder, baking soda, and salt.
3. In a separate bowl, whisk together the eggs, vegetable oil, milk, and vanilla extract.
4. Pour the wet ingredients into the dry ingredients and mix until just combined. Do not overmix.
5. Gently fold in the mixed berries.
6. Fill the muffin cups 2/3 full with the batter.
7. Bake for 20-25 minutes, or until a toothpick inserted into the center of a muffin comes out clean.
8. Let the muffins cool in the tin for 5 minutes, then remove them and let them cool completely on a wire rack.

Nutritional Information: Per serving (1 muffin): 220 calories, 4g protein, 30g carbohydrates, 10g fat, 2g fiber, 35mg cholesterol, 210mg sodium, 100mg potassium.

Vegetable and Egg Muffins

Yield: 6 servings | Prep time: 15 minutes | Cook time: 25 minutes

Ingredients:

- 6 large eggs
- 100g bell peppers (red and yellow), finely diced
- 60g mushrooms, finely diced
- 60g spinach, finely chopped
- 1 small onion, finely diced
- 2 tbsp cheddar cheese, shredded (optional)
- 1/4 tsp salt (or to taste)
- 1/4 tsp black pepper (or to taste)
- Cooking spray or olive oil for greasing

Directions:

1. Preheat the oven to 180°C (350°F). Grease a muffin tin with cooking spray or olive oil.
2. In a medium-sized mixing bowl, whisk the eggs until well beaten. Add the diced vegetables, salt, and pepper to the bowl and stir to combine.
3. Spoon the egg and vegetable mixture into the greased muffin cups, filling each cup almost to the top.
4. Sprinkle a small amount of shredded cheddar cheese over each muffin cup, if desired.
5. Bake for 25 minutes, or until the muffins are set and the tops are slightly browned.
6. Let the muffins cool for a few minutes before removing them from the tin.

Nutritional Information: Per serving: 100 calories, 8g protein, 4g carbohydrates, 6g fat, 1g fiber, 185mg cholesterol, 150mg sodium, 180mg potassium.

Cottage Cheese and Pineapple Bowl

Yield: 2 servings | Prep time: 5 minutes | Cook time: 0 minutes

Ingredients:

- 200g low-fat cottage cheese
- 100g pineapple, cut into small chunks
- 2 tbsp honey
- 2 tbsp chopped walnuts
- 2 tsp chia seeds

Directions:

1. Divide the cottage cheese into two serving bowls.
2. Top each bowl with half of the pineapple chunks.
3. Drizzle 1 tablespoon of honey over the pineapple in each bowl.
4. Sprinkle 1 tablespoon of chopped walnuts and 1 teaspoon of chia seeds over the top of each bowl.
5. Serve immediately and enjoy!

Nutritional Information: Per serving: 210 calories, 14g protein, 27g carbohydrates, 6g fat, 3g fiber, 5mg cholesterol, 380mg sodium, 240mg potassium.

Scrambled Eggs with Sautéed Spinach

Yield: 4 servings | Prep time: 5 minutes | Cook time: 10 minutes

Ingredients:

- 8 large eggs
- 200g fresh spinach leaves
- 2 tbsp olive oil
- Salt and pepper, to taste

Directions:

1. Heat 1 tablespoon of olive oil in a large non-stick skillet over medium heat. Add the spinach leaves and sauté until wilted, about 3-4 minutes. Remove from heat and set aside.
2. In a large bowl, whisk together the eggs, salt, and pepper.
3. Heat the remaining tablespoon of olive oil in the skillet over medium heat. Pour in the whisked eggs and cook, stirring frequently, until the eggs are scrambled and cooked through.
4. Serve the scrambled eggs with the sautéed spinach on the side.

Nutritional Information: Per serving: 180 calories, 12g protein, 3g carbohydrates, 14g fat, 1g fiber, 372mg cholesterol, 130mg sodium, 324mg potassium

Baked Apples with Cinnamon and Honey

Yield: 4 servings | Prep time: 10 minutes | Cook time: 30 minutes

Ingredients:

- 4 medium-sized apples
- 4 tsp honey
- 2 tsp ground cinnamon
- 4 tbsp water

Directions:

1. Preheat your oven to 180°C (350°F).
2. Wash, core, and cut a thin slice off the top of each apple.
3. In a small bowl, mix together honey and cinnamon.
4. Place apples in a baking dish and spoon the cinnamon-honey mixture into the core of each apple.
5. Pour the water into the bottom of the baking dish.
6. Cover the dish with foil and bake for 30 minutes, or until the apples are soft.
7. Serve warm, drizzling any syrup from the dish over the apples.

Nutritional Information: Per serving: 95 calories, 0g protein, 26g carbohydrates, 0g fat, 4g fiber, 0mg cholesterol, 2mg sodium, 140mg potassium.

Almond Butter and Apple Toast

Yield: 2 servings | Prep time: 5 minutes | Cook time: 2 minutes

Ingredients:

- 4 slices of whole grain bread
- 4 tbsp almond butter
- 1 medium apple, thinly sliced
- 2 tsp honey
- A sprinkle of cinnamon (optional)

Directions:

1. Toast the whole grain bread until it is crispy and golden brown.
2. Spread 1 tablespoon of almond butter on each slice of toast.
3. Arrange the thinly sliced apples on top of the almond butter.
4. Drizzle each slice with 1/2 teaspoon of honey.
5. Sprinkle a pinch of cinnamon over the apples, if desired.
6. Serve immediately and enjoy!

Nutritional Information: Per serving: 320 calories, 10g protein, 42g carbohydrates, 14g fat, 7g fiber, 0mg cholesterol, 240mg sodium, 220mg potassium.

Lunchtime Favorites

Lentil and Vegetable Soup

Yield: 4 servings | Prep time: 10 minutes | Cook time: 30 minutes

Ingredients:

- 150g dried lentils, rinsed and drained
- 1 large carrot, chopped
- 1 large onion, chopped
- 2 cloves garlic, minced
- 1 small zucchini, chopped
- 1 tablespoon olive oil
- 1 teaspoon dried thyme
- 1/2 teaspoon ground black pepper
- 1 litre low-sodium vegetable broth
- 2 tablespoons fresh parsley, chopped

Directions:

1. In a large pot, heat the olive oil over medium heat. Add the onions and garlic and sauté until translucent, about 4-5 minutes.
2. Add the carrots, zucchini, and lentils to the pot. Stir in the thyme and pepper.
3. Pour in the low-sodium vegetable broth and bring to a boil. Reduce heat and let simmer for 25-30 minutes, or until the lentils are tender.
4. Stir in the parsley and serve hot.

Nutritional Information: Per serving: 180 calories, 9g protein, 30g carbohydrates, 3g fat, 8g fiber, 0mg cholesterol, 80mg sodium, 580mg potassium.

Turkey and Veggie Wrap with Tzatziki Sauce

Yield: 4 servings | Prep time: 20 minutes | Cook time: 0 minutes

Ingredients:

For the wraps:

- 4 large whole wheat tortillas (about 20cm in diameter)
- 200 grams cooked turkey breast, thinly sliced
- 1 cucumber, thinly sliced
- 1 red bell pepper, thinly sliced
- 1 carrot, peeled and grated
- 50 grams baby spinach leaves
- Salt and pepper, to taste

For the tzatziki sauce:

- 150 grams Greek yogurt
- 1 small cucumber, grated and squeezed to remove excess water
- 2 garlic cloves, minced
- 1 tablespoon fresh dill, chopped
- 1 tablespoon fresh lemon juice
- Salt and pepper, to taste

Directions:

1. In a small bowl, combine all the tzatziki sauce ingredients and mix until well combined. Season with salt and pepper to taste, and refrigerate until ready to use.
2. Lay the tortillas flat on a clean surface. Spread 2 tablespoons of tzatziki sauce on each tortilla.
3. Layer the turkey, cucumber, bell pepper, carrot, and spinach on top of the tzatziki sauce on each tortilla. Season with salt and pepper.
4. Roll the tortillas tightly, tucking in the sides as you roll. Cut the wraps in half and serve with extra tzatziki sauce on the side.

Nutritional Information: Per serving: 280 calories, 18g protein, 35g carbohydrates, 8g fat, 5g fiber, 35mg cholesterol, 670mg sodium, 450mg potassium.

Tomato and Basil Bruschetta

Yield: 4 servings | Prep time: 15 minutes | Cook time: 5 minutes

Ingredients:

- 4 slices of low-sodium whole grain bread
- 2 medium ripe tomatoes, diced
- 1/4 cup fresh basil leaves, finely chopped
- 1 small red onion, finely chopped
- 1 clove garlic, minced
- 1 tablespoon extra-virgin olive oil
- 1 tablespoon balsamic vinegar
- 1/4 teaspoon black pepper

Directions:

1. In a medium-sized bowl, combine the tomatoes, basil, red onion, garlic, olive oil, balsamic vinegar, and black pepper. Mix gently to combine the ingredients.
2. Toast the slices of bread in the oven or on a griddle until they are golden brown and crispy.
3. Spoon the tomato mixture onto each slice of toasted bread, dividing it evenly among the slices.
4. Serve the bruschetta immediately as an appetizer or a light snack.

Nutritional Information: Per serving: 120 calories, 4g protein, 18g carbohydrates, 4g fat, 3g fiber, 0mg cholesterol, 150mg sodium, 200mg potassium.

Asian Chicken Salad with Sesame Dressing

Yield: 4 servings | Prep time: 20 minutes | Cook time: 0 minutes

Ingredients:

For the salad:

- 300 grams cooked chicken breast, shredded
- 150 grams mixed salad greens
- 1 large carrot, peeled and julienned
- 1 red bell pepper, thinly sliced
- 4 spring onions, thinly sliced
- 2 tablespoons fresh coriander, chopped
- 1 tablespoon sesame seeds, toasted

For the sesame dressing:

- 3 tablespoons low-sodium soy sauce
- 2 tablespoons rice vinegar
- 1 tablespoon sesame oil
- 1 tablespoon honey
- 1 garlic clove, minced
- 1 teaspoon fresh ginger, minced
- 1 tablespoon sesame seeds, toasted
- Salt and pepper, to taste

Directions:

1. In a large bowl, combine the salad greens, carrot, bell pepper, spring onions, and coriander.
2. In a small bowl, whisk together all the dressing ingredients until well combined. Season with salt and pepper to taste.
3. Add the shredded chicken to the salad mixture and drizzle with the dressing. Toss until well combined.
4. Divide the salad among 4 serving plates, sprinkle with toasted sesame seeds, and serve.

Nutritional Information: Per serving: 260 calories, 25g protein, 15g carbohydrates, 11g fat, 3g fiber, 55mg cholesterol, 480mg sodium, 420mg potassium.

Tuna Salad with Lemon Vinaigrette

Yield: 4 servings | Prep time: 10 minutes | Cook time: 0 minutes

Ingredients:

- 200g canned tuna in water, drained
- 4 cups mixed salad greens (lettuce, spinach, rocket, etc.)
- 1 medium cucumber, thinly sliced
- 1 medium red bell pepper, thinly sliced
- 1 medium carrot, grated
- 1/4 cup red onion, thinly sliced
- 2 tablespoons olive oil
- 1 tablespoon fresh lemon juice
- 1 teaspoon Dijon mustard
- 1/4 teaspoon ground black pepper
- 1 tablespoon fresh parsley, chopped
- 1 tablespoon fresh dill, chopped

Directions:

1. In a large bowl, combine the salad greens, cucumber, bell pepper, carrot, and onion. Toss to combine.
2. In a small bowl, whisk together the olive oil, lemon juice, Dijon mustard, black pepper, parsley, and dill to create the vinaigrette.
3. Divide the salad among 4 plates. Top each with an equal amount of tuna.
4. Drizzle the vinaigrette over each salad before serving.

Nutritional Information: Per serving: 140 calories, 18g protein, 8g carbohydrates, 5g fat, 2g fiber, 25mg cholesterol, 240mg sodium, 450mg potassium.

Chicken and Rice Casserole

Yield: 4 servings | Prep time: 10 minutes | Cook time: 45 minutes

Ingredients:

- 200g long-grain white rice
- 2 skinless, boneless chicken breasts (about 300g)
- 1 tablespoon olive oil
- 1 small onion, diced
- 1 bell pepper, diced
- 1 medium zucchini, diced
- 1/2 teaspoon black pepper
- 1/2 teaspoon dried thyme
- 1/2 teaspoon dried basil
- 750ml low-sodium chicken broth
- 50g low-sodium cheddar cheese, grated

Directions:

1. Preheat your oven to 190°C (375°F).
2. In a large ovenproof casserole dish, heat the olive oil over medium heat. Add the onion, bell pepper, and zucchini, and sauté until the onion is translucent, about 3-4 minutes.
3. Season the chicken breasts with black pepper, dried thyme, and dried basil. Add the chicken to the casserole dish and brown each side for 2-3 minutes.
4. Add the rice and low-sodium chicken broth to the casserole dish. Stir to combine the ingredients.
5. Cover the casserole dish with foil or a lid, and transfer it to the preheated oven. Bake for 35-40 minutes, or until the rice is cooked through and the chicken is fully cooked.
6. Remove the casserole from the oven, sprinkle the grated cheese over the top, and return it to the oven for 5 minutes to melt the cheese.
7. Serve hot.

Nutritional Information: Per serving: 370 calories, 28g protein, 46g carbohydrates, 7g fat, 2g fiber, 70mg cholesterol, 260mg sodium, 480mg potassium.

Grilled Chicken Caesar Salad

Yield: 4 servings | Prep time: 15 minutes | Cook time: 10 minutes

Ingredients:

- 2 boneless, skinless chicken breasts (about 200g each)
- 1 tablespoon olive oil
- 1/2 teaspoon black pepper
- 4 cups Romaine lettuce, chopped
- 1/4 cup red onion, thinly sliced
- 4 tablespoons low-sodium Caesar dressing
- 4 tablespoons grated Parmesan cheese

Directions:

1. Preheat the grill to medium-high heat. Rub the chicken breasts with olive oil and season with black pepper. Grill the chicken for about 5 minutes on each side, or until cooked through. Remove from the grill and let it rest for a few minutes. Then slice into thin strips.
2. In a large bowl, toss together the Romaine lettuce and red onion. Divide the salad among 4 serving plates.
3. Top each salad with the grilled chicken, Caesar dressing, and grated Parmesan cheese.
4. Serve immediately.

Nutritional Information: Per serving: 220 calories, 30g protein, 5g carbohydrates, 9g fat, 2g fiber, 70mg cholesterol, 320mg sodium, 350mg potassium.

Butternut Squash and Carrot Soup

Yield: 4 servings | Prep time: 10 minutes | Cook time: 30 minutes

Ingredients:

- 500g butternut squash, peeled and cubed
- 300g carrots, peeled and sliced
- 1 small onion, chopped
- 2 cloves garlic, minced
- 1 tablespoon olive oil
- 1/2 teaspoon black pepper
- 1/2 teaspoon dried thyme
- 750ml low-sodium vegetable broth

Directions:

1. In a large pot, heat the olive oil over medium heat. Add the onion and garlic, and sauté until translucent.
2. Add the butternut squash, carrots, black pepper, and dried thyme. Stir to coat the vegetables with the seasonings.
3. Add the low-sodium vegetable broth and bring to a simmer. Cover and cook for 25-30 minutes, or until the vegetables are tender.
4. Use an immersion blender to purée the soup until smooth. Alternatively, you can transfer the soup to a blender and purée it in batches.
5. Serve hot.

Nutritional Information: Per serving: 110 calories, 2g protein, 27g carbohydrates, 3g fat, 5g fiber, 0mg cholesterol, 220mg sodium, 480mg potassium.

Roasted Veggie Quinoa Salad

Yield: 4 servings | Prep time: 15 minutes | Cook time: 30 minutes

Ingredients:

- 150g quinoa, rinsed and drained
- 300ml low-sodium vegetable broth
- 1 small zucchini, chopped
- 1 red bell pepper, chopped
- 1 yellow bell pepper, chopped
- 1 small red onion, chopped
- 1 tablespoon olive oil
- 1/2 teaspoon black pepper
- 2 tablespoons fresh lemon juice
- 1 tablespoon fresh basil, chopped
- 1 tablespoon fresh parsley, chopped

Directions:

1. Preheat your oven to 220°C (425°F).
2. Toss the zucchini, red and yellow bell peppers, and red onion with olive oil and black pepper. Spread the vegetables on a baking sheet and roast for 25-30 minutes, or until the vegetables are tender and slightly browned.
3. While the vegetables are roasting, bring the low-sodium vegetable broth to a boil in a medium saucepan. Add the quinoa, reduce the heat to low, cover, and simmer for 15 minutes, or until the quinoa is cooked through and the liquid is absorbed.
4. In a large bowl, combine the roasted vegetables, cooked quinoa, lemon juice, basil, and parsley. Toss to combine.
5. Serve the salad warm or chilled.

Nutritional Information: Per serving: 200 calories, 7g protein, 35g carbohydrates, 5g fat, 4g fiber, 0mg cholesterol, 80mg sodium, 400mg potassium.

Grilled Eggplant and Zucchini Sandwich

Yield: 4 servings | Prep time: 10 minutes | Cook time: 10 minutes

Ingredients:

- 1 medium eggplant, sliced into 8 rounds (about 1 cm thick)
- 2 medium zucchinis, sliced lengthwise into 8 thin strips
- 4 low-sodium whole grain rolls or baguettes
- 1/4 cup low-sodium hummus
- 1 small red onion, thinly sliced
- 1/4 cup fresh basil leaves
- 1 tablespoon olive oil
- 1/4 teaspoon black pepper

Directions:

1. Preheat a grill or grill pan to medium-high heat. Lightly brush the eggplant and zucchini slices with olive oil and sprinkle with black pepper.
2. Grill the eggplant and zucchini slices for about 3-4 minutes on each side, or until they are tender and have grill marks.
3. Slice the rolls or baguettes in half and spread a thin layer of hummus on the inside of each one.
4. Layer the grilled eggplant, zucchini, red onion slices, and fresh basil leaves onto the bottom half of each roll or baguette.
5. Top with the other half of the roll or baguette and press down gently to secure the sandwich.
6. Serve immediately, or wrap in parchment paper or foil for a portable lunch option.

Nutritional Information: Per serving: 210 calories, 8g protein, 36g carbohydrates, 6g fat, 8g fiber, 0mg cholesterol, 300mg sodium, 450mg potassium.

Shrimp and Rice Noodle Salad

Yield: 4 servings | Prep time: 15 minutes | Cook time: 5 minutes

Ingredients:

- 200 grams rice noodles
- 300 grams cooked and peeled shrimp
- 1 medium cucumber, thinly sliced
- 1 medium carrot, julienned
- 4 spring onions, thinly sliced
- 1/4 cup fresh coriander leaves, chopped
- 1/4 cup fresh mint leaves, chopped
- 1 lime, juiced
- 1 tablespoon fish sauce (low sodium)
- 1 tablespoon rice vinegar
- 1 tablespoon olive oil
- 1 teaspoon honey

Directions:

1. Cook the rice noodles according to the package instructions. Drain and rinse with cold water, then set aside to cool.
2. In a large mixing bowl, combine the shrimp, cucumber, carrot, spring onions, coriander, and mint leaves.
3. In a small bowl, whisk together the lime juice, fish sauce, rice vinegar, olive oil, and honey to make the dressing.
4. Pour the dressing over the shrimp and vegetable mixture and toss to coat.
5. Divide the rice noodles among four serving bowls and top with the shrimp and vegetable mixture.
6. Serve immediately, garnished with additional coriander and mint leaves if desired.

Nutritional Information: Per serving: 270 calories, 17g protein, 42g carbohydrates, 4g fat, 2g fiber, 120mg cholesterol, 350mg sodium, 400mg potassium.

Mediterranean Couscous Salad

Yield: 4 servings | Prep time: 15 minutes | Cook time: 10 minutes

Ingredients:

- 150 grams couscous
- 240 ml low-sodium vegetable broth
- 1 medium red bell pepper, diced
- 1 medium cucumber, diced
- 10 cherry tomatoes, halved
- 50 grams feta cheese, crumbled
- 15 black olives, pitted and sliced
- 2 tablespoons olive oil
- 1 tablespoon red wine vinegar
- 1 tablespoon lemon juice
- 1 teaspoon dried oregano
- 1/4 teaspoon black pepper

Directions:

1. In a medium saucepan, bring the vegetable broth to a boil. Stir in the couscous, remove from heat, cover and let sit for 5 minutes. Fluff with a fork and let it cool.
2. In a large bowl, combine the cooked couscous, red bell pepper, cucumber, cherry tomatoes, feta cheese, and black olives.
3. In a small bowl, whisk together the olive oil, red wine vinegar, lemon juice, oregano, and black pepper. Pour the dressing over the salad and toss to coat.
4. Serve immediately or refrigerate for later use.

Nutritional Information: Per serving: 250 calories, 8g protein, 38g carbohydrates, 8g fat, 4g fiber, 15mg cholesterol, 300mg sodium, 350mg potassium.

Salmon and Asparagus Salad

Yield: 4 servings | Prep time: 15 minutes | Cook time: 15 minutes

Ingredients:

- 4 salmon fillets (approximately 150 grams each)
- 400 grams asparagus, trimmed
- 200 grams mixed salad leaves (e.g. lettuce, spinach, arugula)
- 1 medium red onion, thinly sliced
- 1 tablespoon olive oil
- 1 tablespoon lemon juice
- 1 teaspoon Dijon mustard
- 1/4 teaspoon black pepper

Directions:

1. Preheat your oven to 180°C (350°F). Place the salmon fillets on a baking tray lined with parchment paper, and bake for 12-15 minutes, until the salmon is cooked through and flakes easily with a fork.
2. While the salmon is baking, bring a large pot of water to a boil. Add the asparagus and cook for 3-4 minutes, until tender but still crisp. Drain the asparagus and rinse with cold water to stop the cooking process.
3. In a large bowl, combine the mixed salad leaves, red onion, and asparagus.
4. In a small bowl, whisk together the olive oil, lemon juice, Dijon mustard, and black pepper. Drizzle the dressing over the salad and toss to coat.
5. Serve the salad on individual plates, topped with the baked salmon fillets.

Nutritional Information: Per serving: 260 calories, 28g protein, 10g carbohydrates, 12g fat, 4g fiber, 70mg cholesterol, 220mg sodium, 600mg potassium.

Grilled Turkey and Cranberry Sandwich

Yield: 4 servings | Prep time: 10 minutes | Cook time: 10 minutes

Ingredients:

- 8 slices whole grain bread
- 400 grams turkey breast, cooked and thinly sliced
- 100 grams cranberry sauce, low-sodium
- 100 grams lettuce
- 1 small red onion, thinly sliced
- 2 tablespoons mayonnaise, low-sodium
- 1 tablespoon olive oil

Directions:

1. Preheat a grill or griddle over medium heat.
2. Spread a thin layer of mayonnaise on one side of each slice of bread. On the other side of 4 slices, spread a thin layer of cranberry sauce.
3. Assemble each sandwich by placing the turkey slices, lettuce, and onion on top of the cranberry sauce. Top with the remaining slices of bread, mayonnaise side facing out.
4. Lightly brush the grill or griddle with olive oil. Place the sandwiches on the grill or griddle and cook for 4-5 minutes on each side, until the bread is golden brown and the turkey is heated through.
5. Remove the sandwiches from the grill or griddle, let them cool slightly, and then slice in half. Serve immediately.

Nutritional Information: Per serving: 310 calories, 30g protein, 32g carbohydrates, 9g fat, 5g fiber, 55mg cholesterol, 270mg sodium, 350mg potassium.

Spinach and Mushroom Quesadilla

Yield: 4 servings | Prep time: 10 minutes | Cook time: 15 minutes

Ingredients:

- 4 whole wheat tortillas (about 20 cm diameter)
- 200 grams fresh spinach, washed and chopped
- 200 grams mushrooms, sliced
- 1 small onion, chopped
- 2 cloves garlic, minced
- 100 grams shredded mozzarella cheese
- 1 tablespoon olive oil
- 1/2 teaspoon black pepper

Directions:

1. In a large skillet, heat olive oil over medium heat. Add onion and garlic and sauté until onion is translucent, about 2 minutes.
2. Add mushrooms and continue sautéing for another 5 minutes, until mushrooms are tender.
3. Add spinach and sauté for 2 more minutes, until spinach is wilted. Season with black pepper.
4. Preheat another skillet over medium heat. Place a tortilla in the skillet and sprinkle with a quarter of the shredded cheese.
5. Spoon a quarter of the spinach and mushroom mixture onto one half of the tortilla. Fold the other half over the filling and press down gently.
6. Cook for 2-3 minutes on each side, until the tortilla is golden brown and the cheese is melted.
7. Remove from the skillet and cut into wedges. Repeat with remaining tortillas and filling. Serve immediately.

Nutritional Information: Per serving: 250 calories, 11g protein, 30g carbohydrates, 11g fat, 5g fiber, 20mg cholesterol, 300mg sodium, 350mg potassium.

Creamy Carrot and Parsnip Soup

Yield: 4 servings | Prep time: 10 minutes | Cook time: 30 minutes

Ingredients:

- 300 grams carrots, peeled and chopped
- 300 grams parsnips, peeled and chopped
- 1 small onion, chopped
- 2 cloves garlic, minced
- 1 litre low-sodium vegetable broth
- 150 ml low-fat cream
- 1 tablespoon olive oil
- 1/2 teaspoon dried thyme
- 1/4 teaspoon black pepper

Directions:

1. In a large pot, heat olive oil over medium heat. Add onions and garlic and sauté until onions are translucent, about 3 minutes.
2. Add carrots and parsnips, and continue sautéing for another 5 minutes.
3. Pour in the vegetable broth, thyme, and black pepper. Bring to a boil, then reduce heat to low and simmer for 20 minutes, until vegetables are tender.
4. Remove from heat and let it cool slightly. Use an immersion blender or a regular blender to blend the soup until smooth.
5. Return soup to the pot and stir in the cream. Heat over low heat until heated through. Serve hot.

Nutritional Information: Per serving: 170 calories, 3g protein, 29g carbohydrates, 6g fat, 7g fiber, 15mg cholesterol, 180mg sodium, 500mg potassium.

Baked Chicken and Vegetable Stir-Fry

Yield: 4 servings | Prep time: 15 minutes | Cook time: 25 minutes

Ingredients:

- 400 grams boneless, skinless chicken breast, cut into bite-sized pieces
- 200 grams broccoli florets
- 150 grams bell peppers, sliced
- 150 grams carrots, sliced
- 150 grams snow peas
- 2 cloves garlic, minced
- 2 tablespoons low-sodium soy sauce
- 1 tablespoon olive oil
- 1 teaspoon ginger, minced
- 1 teaspoon cornflour
- 1 tablespoon water
- 1/2 teaspoon black pepper

Directions:

1. Preheat your oven to 200°C (400°F). In a large bowl, toss together chicken, broccoli, bell peppers, carrots, and snow peas with olive oil, garlic, and ginger.
2. In a small bowl, whisk together low-sodium soy sauce, cornflour, water, and black pepper until smooth.
3. Pour sauce over chicken and vegetables, tossing to coat. Spread out onto a baking sheet in an even layer.
4. Bake for 20-25 minutes, stirring once halfway through, until chicken is cooked through and vegetables are tender.
5. Serve hot, on its own or with cooked rice.

Nutritional Information: Per serving: 180 calories, 25g protein, 15g carbohydrates, 4g fat, 4g fiber, 55mg cholesterol, 320mg sodium, 580mg potassium.

Greek Salad with Feta Cheese

Yield: 4 servings | Prep time: 15 minutes | Cook time: 0 minutes

Ingredients:

- 200 grams cherry tomatoes, halved
- 1 large cucumber, diced
- 1 red onion, thinly sliced
- 1 green bell pepper, sliced
- 150 grams feta cheese, crumbled
- 50 grams Kalamata olives, pitted and sliced
- 2 tablespoons extra virgin olive oil
- 1 tablespoon red wine vinegar
- 1 teaspoon dried oregano
- 1/2 teaspoon black pepper

Directions:

1. In a large bowl, combine cherry tomatoes, cucumber, red onion, green bell pepper, feta cheese, and Kalamata olives.
2. In a small bowl, whisk together olive oil, red wine vinegar, oregano, and black pepper until well combined.
3. Drizzle the dressing over the salad and toss gently to coat.
4. Serve immediately, or cover and refrigerate for 1-2 hours to allow the flavors to meld.

Nutritional Information: Per serving: 170 calories, 6g protein, 11g carbohydrates, 12g fat, 3g fiber, 22mg cholesterol, 550mg sodium, 350mg potassium.

Turkey and Avocado Wraps

Yield: 4 servings | Prep time: 10 minutes | Cook time: 0 minutes

Ingredients:

- 4 large whole-wheat tortillas (about 25cm in diameter)
- 200g cooked turkey breast, sliced
- 1 medium avocado, sliced
- 1 cup baby spinach leaves
- 1 medium tomato, thinly sliced
- 1/4 cup red onion, thinly sliced
- 2 tablespoons low-fat mayonnaise
- 1 tablespoon Dijon mustard
- 1/2 teaspoon black pepper

Directions:

1. In a small bowl, mix together the low-fat mayonnaise and Dijon mustard. Season with black pepper and stir until well combined.
2. Lay out the tortillas on a clean surface. Spread each tortilla with the mayonnaise and mustard mixture.
3. Evenly distribute the turkey, avocado, spinach, tomato, and onion among the tortillas.
4. Roll each tortilla tightly around the fillings, tucking in the sides as you go, to create a wrap.
5. Slice each wrap in half and serve.

Nutritional Information: Per serving: 250 calories, 15g protein, 30g carbohydrates, 10g fat, 5g fiber, 30mg cholesterol, 400mg sodium, 350mg potassium.

Dinner Classics

Garlic Lemon Herb Roast Chicken

Yield: 4 servings | Prep time: 15 minutes | Cook time: 45 minutes

Ingredients:

- 1 whole chicken (about 1.5 kilograms)
- 1 lemon, zest and juice
- 4 garlic cloves, minced
- 2 tablespoons fresh rosemary, finely chopped
- 2 tablespoons fresh thyme, finely chopped
- 2 tablespoons olive oil
- Salt and pepper, to taste
- 100 milliliters low-sodium chicken broth

Directions:

1. Preheat your oven to 190°C (375°F).
2. In a small bowl, mix together the lemon zest, lemon juice, garlic, rosemary, thyme, olive oil, salt, and pepper to make the herb mixture.
3. Clean the chicken and pat it dry with paper towels. Season the inside of the chicken with salt and pepper.
4. Rub the herb mixture all over the chicken, inside and out. Place the chicken on a roasting rack set inside a roasting pan.
5. Pour the low-sodium chicken broth into the bottom of the roasting pan.
6. Roast the chicken in the preheated oven for about 45 minutes, or until the internal temperature reaches 75°C (165°F) and the juices run clear. Remove from the oven and let rest for 10 minutes before carving.

Nutritional Information: Per serving: 420 calories, 30g protein, 3g carbohydrates, 31g fat, 1g fiber, 105mg cholesterol, 230mg sodium, 390mg potassium.

Oven-Baked Cod with Cherry Tomatoes

Yield: 4 servings | Prep time: 10 minutes | Cook time: 20 minutes

Ingredients:

- 4 cod fillets (about 150 grams each)
- 250 grams cherry tomatoes, halved
- 2 tablespoons olive oil
- 2 cloves garlic, minced
- 1 teaspoon dried oregano
- 1 teaspoon dried basil
- Salt and pepper, to taste
- Fresh parsley, chopped for garnish

Directions:

1. Preheat the oven to 200°C (390°F). Grease a baking dish with a little olive oil.
2. In a medium-sized bowl, mix together the cherry tomatoes, olive oil, garlic, oregano, and basil. Season with salt and pepper to taste.
3. Place the cod fillets in the baking dish and top with the tomato mixture.
4. Bake in the oven for 18-20 minutes or until the fish flakes easily with a fork.
5. Garnish with fresh parsley and serve.

Nutritional Information: Per serving: 180 calories, 25g protein, 4g carbohydrates, 7g fat, 1g fiber, 60mg cholesterol, 95mg sodium, 500mg potassium.

Beef Stew with Carrots and Celery

Yield: 4 servings | Prep time: 15 minutes | Cook time: 2 hours

Ingredients:

- 500 grams lean beef stew meat, cut into bite-sized pieces
- 2 tablespoons olive oil
- 1 onion, chopped
- 2 cloves garlic, minced
- 4 medium carrots, peeled and sliced
- 4 celery stalks, sliced
- 1 teaspoon dried thyme
- 1 bay leaf
- Salt and pepper, to taste
- 750 mL low-sodium beef broth
- 2 tablespoons cornstarch
- 60 mL cold water

Directions:

1. In a large pot, heat the olive oil over medium-high heat. Add the beef and brown on all sides, then remove from the pot and set aside.
2. Add the onion and garlic to the pot and sauté until the onion is translucent.
3. Return the beef to the pot and add the carrots, celery, thyme, bay leaf, salt, and pepper. Stir to combine.
4. Pour in the low-sodium beef broth and bring to a simmer. Reduce the heat to low, cover the pot, and let it simmer for 1.5 hours, stirring occasionally.
5. In a small bowl, mix together the cornstarch and cold water until smooth. Add this to the pot and stir to thicken the stew. Simmer for an additional 15 minutes, uncovered, until the vegetables are tender and the stew is thickened.
6. Remove the bay leaf before serving.

Nutritional Information: Per serving: 315 calories, 32g protein, 17g carbohydrates, 12g fat, 3g fiber, 80mg cholesterol, 480mg sodium, 700mg potassium.

Rosemary and Lemon Grilled Chicken

Yield: 4 servings | Prep time: 15 minutes | Cook time: 15 minutes

Ingredients:

- 4 boneless, skinless chicken breasts (about 500 grams)
- 2 tablespoons olive oil
- 2 tablespoons fresh lemon juice
- 2 teaspoons fresh rosemary, minced
- 1 clove garlic, minced
- Salt and pepper, to taste

Directions:

1. In a large bowl, whisk together the olive oil, lemon juice, rosemary, garlic, salt, and pepper. Add the chicken breasts, turning to coat them in the marinade. Cover and refrigerate for at least 30 minutes, or up to 4 hours.
2. Preheat the grill to medium-high heat. Remove the chicken from the marinade, letting any excess drip off.
3. Grill the chicken for 6-7 minutes on each side, or until the internal temperature reaches 75°C (165°F) and the chicken is cooked through.
4. Remove the chicken from the grill and let it rest for a few minutes before serving.

Nutritional Information: Per serving: 210 calories, 29g protein, 2g carbohydrates, 9g fat, 0g fiber, 80mg cholesterol, 75mg sodium, 250mg potassium.

Baked Tilapia with Salsa Verde

Yield: 4 servings | Prep time: 15 minutes | Cook time: 20 minutes

Ingredients:

- 4 tilapia fillets (about 500 grams)
- 1 tablespoon olive oil
- Salt and pepper, to taste

For the Salsa Verde:

- 1 small bunch of fresh parsley, finely chopped (about 30 grams)
- 2 tablespoons capers, rinsed and chopped
- 1 clove garlic, minced
- 1 tablespoon fresh lemon juice
- 1/2 teaspoon lemon zest
- 1/4 teaspoon red pepper flakes (optional)
- 3 tablespoons olive oil

Directions:

1. Preheat the oven to 180°C (350°F). Place the tilapia fillets on a baking sheet lined with parchment paper or foil. Drizzle with olive oil, season with salt and pepper, and bake for 12-15 minutes, or until the fish flakes easily with a fork.
2. While the tilapia is baking, make the salsa verde. In a small bowl, combine the parsley, capers, garlic, lemon juice, lemon zest, and red pepper flakes (if using). Gradually whisk in the olive oil until combined. Season with salt and pepper to taste.
3. Once the tilapia is done baking, remove from the oven and transfer to serving plates. Spoon the salsa verde over the fish, and serve immediately.

Nutritional Information: Per serving: 250 calories, 32g protein, 1g carbohydrates, 12g fat, 0g fiber, 85mg cholesterol, 150mg sodium, 400mg potassium.

Oven-Baked Trout with Almonds

Yield: 4 servings | Prep time: 10 minutes | Cook time: 12 minutes

Ingredients:

- 4 trout fillets (approximately 150 grams each)
- 50 grams of almond slivers
- 2 tablespoons of olive oil
- 1 tablespoon of fresh parsley, chopped
- 1 teaspoon of lemon zest
- 1 tablespoon of lemon juice
- 1/2 teaspoon of salt
- 1/4 teaspoon of black pepper

Directions:

1. Preheat the oven to 200°C (390°F).
2. Arrange the trout fillets skin-side down in a baking dish.
3. In a small bowl, combine the olive oil, parsley, lemon zest, lemon juice, salt, and black pepper. Mix well and brush over the trout fillets.
4. Sprinkle the almond slivers over the trout fillets.
5. Bake in the preheated oven for 10 to 12 minutes or until the trout is cooked through and flakes easily with a fork.
6. Remove from the oven and serve immediately.

Nutritional Information: Per serving: 340 calories, 34g protein, 3g carbohydrates, 22g fat, 2g fiber, 80mg cholesterol, 330mg sodium, 570mg potassium.

Baked Salmon with Dill and Lemon

Yield: 4 servings | Prep time: 10 minutes | Cook time: 20 minutes

Ingredients:

- 4 salmon fillets (about 150 grams each)
- 2 tablespoons fresh dill, finely chopped
- 1 lemon, thinly sliced
- 1 tablespoon olive oil
- Salt and pepper, to taste
- 1 lemon, zest and juice

Directions:

1. Preheat your oven to 180°C (350°F).
2. Place the salmon fillets on a baking sheet lined with parchment paper.
3. In a small bowl, mix together the olive oil, lemon zest, lemon juice, salt, and pepper. Brush this mixture over each salmon fillet.
4. Sprinkle the fresh dill over the salmon fillets and then place 2-3 thin lemon slices on top of each fillet.
5. Bake in the preheated oven for 15-20 minutes, or until the salmon easily flakes with a fork.

Nutritional Information: Per serving: 230 calories, 28g protein, 1g carbohydrates, 12g fat, 0g fiber, 65mg cholesterol, 90mg sodium, 450mg potassium.

Tuscan-Style Beef Stew

Yield: 4 servings | Prep time: 15 minutes | Cook time: 120 minutes

Ingredients:

- 400 grams lean beef stew meat, cut into 3 cm chunks
- 1/2 teaspoon salt
- 1/4 teaspoon black pepper
- 2 tablespoons olive oil
- 1 large onion, chopped
- 3 cloves garlic, minced
- 1 cup (240 ml) low-sodium beef broth
- 1 cup (240 ml) water
- 2 carrots, peeled and sliced into 1 cm rounds
- 2 celery stalks, sliced into 1 cm pieces
- 2 teaspoons dried rosemary
- 1 teaspoon dried thyme
- 2 bay leaves
- 2 tablespoons chopped fresh parsley

Directions:

1. Season the beef chunks with salt and pepper.
2. In a large pot, heat the olive oil over medium-high heat. Add the beef and brown on all sides, about 3-5 minutes. Remove the beef and set aside.
3. In the same pot, add the chopped onion and sauté for 3 minutes, until softened. Add the minced garlic and sauté for an additional 1 minute.
4. Return the browned beef to the pot. Add the beef broth, water, carrots, celery, rosemary, thyme, and bay leaves. Bring to a boil, then reduce the heat to low, cover, and simmer for 2 hours, stirring occasionally, until the beef is tender.
5. Remove the bay leaves and discard. Garnish with chopped parsley before serving.

Nutritional Information: Per serving: 310 calories, 28g protein, 11g carbohydrates, 16g fat, 2g fiber, 80mg cholesterol, 400mg sodium, 580mg potassium.

Grilled Pork Chops with Apple Compote

Yield: 4 servings | Prep time: 10 minutes | Cook time: 30 minutes

Ingredients:

- 4 pork chops (about 200 grams each)
- 2 tablespoons olive oil
- Salt and pepper, to taste

For the Apple Compote:

- 4 medium apples (about 500 grams), peeled, cored and diced
- 1 tablespoon unsalted butter
- 1/2 teaspoon ground cinnamon
- 1 tablespoon lemon juice
- 1/2 teaspoon vanilla extract

Directions:

1. Preheat the grill to medium-high heat. Season the pork chops with olive oil, salt, and pepper on both sides.
2. In a medium saucepan, melt the butter over medium heat. Add the diced apples, cinnamon, lemon juice, and vanilla extract. Stir to combine.
3. Reduce the heat to low, cover, and simmer for 20-25 minutes, stirring occasionally, until the apples are soft and the compote has thickened. Remove from heat.
4. Grill the pork chops for 5-7 minutes on each side, until cooked through and the internal temperature reaches 63°C (145°F).
5. Serve the grilled pork chops with the apple compote on top.

Nutritional Information: Per serving: 425 calories, 30g protein, 30g carbohydrates, 21g fat, 4g fiber, 85mg cholesterol, 105mg sodium, 490mg potassium.

Stuffed Bell Peppers with Ground Turkey

Yield: 4 servings | Prep time: 20 minutes | Cook time: 40 minutes

Ingredients:

- 4 large bell peppers (any colour), tops removed and seeds cleaned out
- 400 grams ground turkey
- 1 small onion, finely chopped
- 2 cloves garlic, minced
- 200 grams cooked brown rice
- 1 medium carrot, grated
- 1 medium zucchini, grated
- 1/2 teaspoon dried oregano
- 1/2 teaspoon dried basil
- 1/4 teaspoon black pepper
- 100 grams low-sodium tomato sauce
- 50 grams shredded low-sodium mozzarella cheese (optional)

Directions:

1. Preheat your oven to 190°C (375°F).
2. In a large skillet over medium heat, sauté the onion and garlic until softened. Add the ground turkey and cook until browned, breaking it up with a spoon as it cooks. Stir in the cooked rice, grated carrot, zucchini, oregano, basil, and black pepper.
3. Remove the skillet from the heat and carefully spoon the turkey and rice mixture into the hollowed-out bell peppers. Place the stuffed peppers in a baking dish, and pour the tomato sauce over the top.
4. Cover the baking dish with foil and bake for 30 minutes. Remove the foil and sprinkle the optional mozzarella cheese over the top of the peppers. Bake for an additional 10 minutes or until the cheese is melted and bubbly. Serve the stuffed peppers hot.

Nutritional Information: Per serving: 300 calories, 25g protein, 30g carbohydrates, 8g fat, 4g fiber, 75mg cholesterol, 170mg sodium, 580mg potassium.

Pan-Seared Tuna Steaks with Capers

Yield: 4 servings | Prep time: 10 minutes | Cook time: 8 minutes

Ingredients:

- 4 tuna steaks (about 150 grams each)
- Salt and pepper, to taste
- 2 tablespoons olive oil
- 2 cloves garlic, minced
- 1/4 cup (60 ml) dry white wine
- 2 tablespoons capers, drained
- 2 tablespoons chopped fresh parsley
- 1 tablespoon lemon juice

Directions:

1. Season the tuna steaks with salt and pepper.
2. In a large skillet, heat the olive oil over medium-high heat. Add the tuna steaks and sear for about 2-3 minutes on each side, or until they reach your desired level of doneness. Remove the tuna steaks from the skillet and set them aside.
3. In the same skillet, add the garlic and cook for about 1 minute, or until it is fragrant.
4. Add the white wine, capers, parsley, and lemon juice to the skillet. Cook for about 2-3 minutes, or until the sauce has reduced slightly.
5. Pour the sauce over the tuna steaks and serve immediately.

Nutritional Information: Per serving: 260 calories, 35g protein, 1g carbohydrates, 12g fat, 0g fiber, 60mg cholesterol, 350mg sodium, 500mg potassium.

Grilled Swordfish with Olive Tapenade

Yield: 4 servings | Prep time: 15 minutes | Cook time: 10 minutes

Ingredients:

- 4 swordfish steaks (approximately 150 grams each)
- 2 tablespoons of olive oil
- 1/4 teaspoon of black pepper
- 1/4 teaspoon of salt

For the tapenade:

- 100 grams of green olives, pitted and chopped
- 100 grams of black olives, pitted and chopped
- 2 cloves of garlic, minced
- 2 tablespoons of capers, drained and chopped
- 2 tablespoons of fresh parsley, chopped
- 1 tablespoon of lemon juice
- 1 tablespoon of olive oil

Directions:

1. Preheat the grill to medium-high heat.
2. Brush the swordfish steaks with olive oil and season with salt and pepper.
3. Grill the swordfish for about 4-5 minutes on each side or until it is cooked through.
4. In a food processor, combine the green olives, black olives, garlic, capers, parsley, lemon juice, and olive oil. Pulse until the ingredients are combined but still chunky.
5. Serve the swordfish steaks topped with the olive tapenade.

Nutritional Information: Per serving: 245 calories, 30g protein, 3g carbohydrates, 12g fat, 2g fiber, 60mg cholesterol, 550mg sodium, 400mg potassium.

Baked Haddock with Lemon Butter Sauce

Yield: 4 servings | Prep time: 10 minutes | Cook time: 20 minutes

Ingredients:

- 4 haddock fillets (about 150 grams each)
- 1/4 teaspoon black pepper
- 1/4 teaspoon salt
- 2 tablespoons unsalted butter
- 2 tablespoons lemon juice
- 2 cloves garlic, minced
- 2 tablespoons fresh parsley, chopped

Directions:

1. Preheat the oven to 180°C (350°F).
2. Season the haddock fillets with salt and pepper and place them in a baking dish.
3. In a small saucepan, melt the butter over medium heat. Add the garlic and sauté for 1 minute.
4. Remove from heat and stir in the lemon juice and half of the parsley.
5. Pour the lemon butter sauce over the haddock fillets.
6. Bake in the preheated oven for 15-20 minutes or until the fish flakes easily with a fork.
7. Garnish with the remaining parsley and serve.

Nutritional Information: Per serving: 200 calories, 25g protein, 1g carbohydrates, 11g fat, 0g fiber, 85mg cholesterol, 230mg sodium, 390mg potassium.

Lemon Herb Grilled Shrimp

Yield: 4 servings | Prep time: 15 minutes | Cook time: 6 minutes

Ingredients:

- 450 grams of raw large shrimp, peeled and deveined
- 1 tablespoon olive oil
- 3 cloves garlic, minced
- 1 tablespoon fresh parsley, chopped
- 1 tablespoon fresh chives, chopped
- Zest and juice of 1 lemon
- 1/2 teaspoon black pepper
- 1/4 teaspoon salt

Directions:

1. Preheat your grill to medium-high heat.
2. In a large bowl, combine the olive oil, garlic, parsley, chives, lemon zest, lemon juice, black pepper, and salt. Mix well to combine.
3. Add the shrimp to the bowl and toss to coat them with the herb mixture. Let the shrimp marinate for 5 to 10 minutes.
4. Thread the shrimp onto skewers, leaving a little space between each shrimp.
5. Place the shrimp skewers on the grill and cook for 2 to 3 minutes on each side, or until the shrimp are pink and opaque.
6. Remove the shrimp skewers from the grill and serve immediately.

Nutritional Information: Per serving: 140 calories, 24g protein, 2g carbohydrates, 4g fat, 0g fiber, 180mg cholesterol, 340mg sodium, 220mg potassium.

Chicken Marsala with Mushrooms

Yield: 4 servings | Prep time: 10 minutes | Cook time: 20 minutes

Ingredients:

- 4 boneless, skinless chicken breasts (approximately 150 grams each)
- 150 grams of button mushrooms, sliced
- 120 ml of Marsala wine
- 1 small onion, chopped
- 2 cloves garlic, minced
- 2 tablespoons of olive oil
- 1 tablespoon of fresh parsley, chopped
- 1/4 teaspoon of black pepper
- 1/4 teaspoon of salt

Directions:

1. In a large skillet, heat the olive oil over medium-high heat.
2. Season the chicken breasts with salt and pepper. Add the chicken to the skillet and cook until browned on both sides, about 3-4 minutes per side. Remove the chicken from the skillet and set aside.
3. In the same skillet, add the onions and garlic and cook until softened, about 2 minutes.
4. Add the mushrooms to the skillet and cook until browned, about 4-5 minutes.
5. Add the Marsala wine to the skillet and bring to a simmer. Return the chicken to the skillet and simmer for 8-10 minutes or until the chicken is cooked through.
6. Remove from the heat, sprinkle with chopped parsley, and serve.

Nutritional Information: Per serving: 285 calories, 28g protein, 8g carbohydrates, 14g fat, 1g fiber, 75mg cholesterol, 220mg sodium, 460mg potassium.

Pork Tenderloin with Dijon Mustard Sauce

Yield: 4 servings | Prep time: 10 minutes | Cook time: 30 minutes

Ingredients:

- 2 pork tenderloins (about 400 grams each)
- 1 tablespoon olive oil
- 1/2 teaspoon black pepper
- 1/4 teaspoon salt

For the sauce:

- 2 tablespoons Dijon mustard
- 1 tablespoon olive oil
- 2 cloves garlic, minced
- 150 ml low-sodium chicken broth
- 2 tablespoons fresh parsley, chopped

Directions:

1. Preheat the oven to 200°C (390°F).
2. Rub the pork tenderloins with olive oil, salt, and pepper.
3. In a large oven-proof skillet, heat 1 tablespoon of olive oil over medium-high heat. Add the pork tenderloins and brown on all sides, about 5 minutes.
4. Transfer the skillet to the preheated oven and roast for 20 minutes or until the internal temperature reaches 63°C (145°F).
5. Remove the pork from the oven and let it rest for 5 minutes. Then slice it into medallions.
6. In a small saucepan, heat 1 tablespoon of olive oil over medium heat. Add the garlic and sauté for 1 minute.
7. Add the Dijon mustard and chicken broth to the saucepan and bring to a simmer. Cook for 2-3 minutes, stirring constantly.
8. Stir in the chopped parsley and serve the sauce over the pork medallions.

Nutritional Information: Per serving: 295 calories, 37g protein, 2g carbohydrates, 15g fat, 0g fiber, 110mg cholesterol, 410mg sodium, 510mg potassium.

Grilled Scallops with Lemon Herb Sauce

Yield: 4 servings | Prep time: 10 minutes | Cook time: 6 minutes

Ingredients:

- 16 large scallops (about 500 grams)
- Salt and pepper, to taste
- 2 tablespoons olive oil
- 1/4 cup (60 ml) fresh lemon juice
- 2 cloves garlic, minced
- 2 tablespoons chopped fresh parsley
- 2 tablespoons chopped fresh basil
- 1 teaspoon dried oregano
- Lemon wedges, for garnish

Directions:

1. Preheat your grill to medium-high heat. Season the scallops with salt and pepper.
2. In a small bowl, mix together the olive oil, lemon juice, garlic, parsley, basil, and oregano.
3. Brush the scallops with a small amount of the lemon herb sauce. Grill the scallops for about 2-3 minutes on each side, or until they are cooked through and have a nice sear.
4. Remove the scallops from the grill and drizzle the remaining lemon herb sauce over them.
5. Serve immediately, garnished with lemon wedges.

Nutritional Information: Per serving: 170 calories, 20g protein, 3g carbohydrates, 9g fat, 0g fiber, 50mg cholesterol, 350mg sodium, 400mg potassium.

Balsamic Glazed Chicken Thighs

Yield: 4 servings | Prep time: 10 minutes | Cook time: 25 minutes

Ingredients:

- 4 boneless, skinless chicken thighs (about 600 grams total)
- Salt and pepper, to taste
- 1 tablespoon olive oil
- 2 cloves garlic, minced
- 1/2 cup (120 ml) balsamic vinegar
- 2 teaspoons brown sugar
- 1 teaspoon dried rosemary
- 1 teaspoon dried thyme

Directions:

1. Season the chicken thighs with salt and pepper.
2. In a large skillet, heat the olive oil over medium-high heat. Add the chicken thighs and cook for about 4-5 minutes on each side, or until they are browned and cooked through. Remove the chicken from the skillet and set it aside.
3. In the same skillet, add the garlic and cook for about 1 minute, or until it is fragrant.
4. Add the balsamic vinegar, brown sugar, rosemary, and thyme to the skillet. Simmer the mixture for about 5-7 minutes, or until it has reduced and thickened into a glaze.
5. Return the chicken to the skillet and spoon the glaze over the chicken. Cook for an additional 2-3 minutes, or until the chicken is heated through and coated with the glaze.

Nutritional Information: Per serving: 250 calories, 28g protein, 10g carbohydrates, 10g fat, 0g fiber, 95mg cholesterol, 270mg sodium, 330mg potassium.

Sides and Snacks

Carrot and Zucchini Fritters

Yield: 4 servings | Prep time: 15 minutes | Cook time: 10 minutes

Ingredients:

- 150 grams carrots, grated
- 150 grams zucchini, grated
- 50 grams onion, finely chopped
- 2 large eggs
- 40 grams all-purpose flour
- Salt and pepper, to taste
- 2 tablespoons olive oil
- 2 tablespoons fresh parsley, chopped

Directions:

1. In a large mixing bowl, combine the grated carrots, zucchini, and chopped onion.
2. In a separate bowl, beat the eggs and then add them to the vegetable mixture. Mix well.
3. Add the flour, salt, and pepper to the vegetable and egg mixture. Stir until well combined.
4. Heat the olive oil in a large frying pan over medium heat.
5. Spoon the mixture into the pan, forming small fritters. Cook for about 3-4 minutes on each side, or until the fritters are golden brown and cooked through.
6. Remove the fritters from the pan and drain them on paper towels. Sprinkle with chopped parsley before serving.

Nutritional Information: Per serving: 170 calories, 6g protein, 15g carbohydrates, 10g fat, 2g fiber, 90mg cholesterol, 100mg sodium, 280mg potassium.

Baked Sweet Potato Fries

Yield: 4 servings | Prep time: 10 minutes | Cook time: 30 minutes

Ingredients:

- 600 grams sweet potatoes, peeled and cut into fries
- 2 tablespoons olive oil
- 1/2 teaspoon salt
- 1/4 teaspoon black pepper
- 1/2 teaspoon paprika
- 2 tablespoons fresh parsley, chopped (optional)

Directions:

1. Preheat your oven to 220°C (425°F). Line a baking sheet with parchment paper.
2. In a large bowl, toss the sweet potato fries with olive oil, salt, pepper, and paprika until evenly coated.
3. Spread the fries in a single layer on the prepared baking sheet, ensuring they are not touching.
4. Bake for 25-30 minutes, turning the fries halfway through, until they are golden brown and crispy.
5. Remove the fries from the oven and sprinkle with chopped parsley, if desired.
6. Serve the baked sweet potato fries immediately as a side dish or snack.

Nutritional Information: Per serving: 215 calories, 2g protein, 37g carbohydrates, 7g fat, 5g fiber, 0mg cholesterol, 330mg sodium, 600mg potassium.

Cucumber and Dill Yogurt Dip

Yield: 4 servings | Prep time: 10 minutes | Cook time: 0 minutes

Ingredients:

- 200 grams plain Greek yogurt
- 1 small cucumber, peeled, seeded, and finely diced (about 150 grams)
- 2 tablespoons fresh dill, chopped
- 1 clove garlic, minced
- 1 tablespoon lemon juice
- 1/4 teaspoon salt
- 1/4 teaspoon black pepper

Directions:

1. In a medium bowl, combine Greek yogurt, cucumber, dill, garlic, lemon juice, salt, and pepper. Stir until all ingredients are well mixed.
2. Cover the bowl with plastic wrap and refrigerate for at least 1 hour, allowing the flavours to meld.
3. Before serving, give the dip a quick stir and adjust seasoning as needed.
4. Serve the cucumber and dill yogurt dip with fresh vegetables, pita bread, or as a sauce for grilled meats.

Nutritional Information: Per serving: 45 calories, 6g protein, 4g carbohydrates, 1g fat, 0.5g fiber, 5mg cholesterol, 165mg sodium, 175mg potassium.

Roasted Cauliflower with Garlic

Yield: 4 servings | Prep time: 10 minutes | Cook time: 25 minutes

Ingredients:

- 1 large cauliflower head (about 600 grams), cut into florets
- 2 tablespoons olive oil
- 4 cloves garlic, minced
- Salt and pepper, to taste
- 2 teaspoons fresh parsley, chopped

Directions:

1. Preheat your oven to 200°C (392°F).
2. In a large mixing bowl, toss the cauliflower florets with the olive oil and minced garlic. Season with salt and pepper.
3. Spread the cauliflower florets on a baking sheet in a single layer.
4. Roast in the oven for about 20-25 minutes, or until the cauliflower is tender and lightly browned. Stir halfway through the cooking time to ensure even roasting.
5. Remove the cauliflower from the oven and sprinkle with fresh parsley.

Nutritional Information: Per serving: 100 calories, 3g protein, 10g carbohydrates, 7g fat, 4g fiber, 0mg cholesterol, 60mg sodium, 400mg potassium.

Garlic Sautéed Spinach

Yield: 4 servings | Prep time: 5 minutes | Cook time: 5 minutes

Ingredients:

- 400 grams fresh spinach leaves, washed and drained
- 3 cloves garlic, minced
- 2 tablespoons olive oil
- 1/4 teaspoon salt
- 1/4 teaspoon black pepper

Directions:

1. Heat the olive oil in a large non-stick skillet over medium heat. Add the minced garlic and sauté for 1-2 minutes, until fragrant but not browned.
2. Add the fresh spinach leaves to the skillet. Using tongs, gently toss the spinach leaves in the oil and garlic mixture until they are well coated.
3. Continue to sauté the spinach for 2-3 minutes, or until the leaves have wilted and reduced in volume. Season with salt and pepper.
4. Remove the skillet from heat and transfer the sautéed spinach to a serving dish. Serve immediately as a side dish or use it as a filling for sandwiches, wraps, or omelettes.

Nutritional Information: Per serving: 65 calories, 2g protein, 3g carbohydrates, 5g fat, 2g fiber, 0mg cholesterol, 215mg sodium, 340mg potassium.

Greek Tzatziki Sauce with Veggies

Yield: 4 servings | Prep time: 15 minutes | Cook time: 0 minutes

Ingredients:

- 300 grams Greek yogurt, full fat
- 1/2 large cucumber, peeled, seeded, and finely grated (about 100 grams)
- 3 cloves garlic, minced
- 2 tablespoons fresh dill, finely chopped
- 1 tablespoon extra virgin olive oil
- 1 tablespoon white vinegar
- 1/4 teaspoon salt
- 1/4 teaspoon black pepper
- 100 grams cherry tomatoes, halved
- 100 grams bell pepper, sliced
- 100 grams carrot sticks

Directions:

1. In a medium-sized bowl, combine Greek yogurt, grated cucumber, minced garlic, chopped dill, olive oil, white vinegar, salt, and black pepper. Mix well until all the ingredients are thoroughly combined.
2. Cover the bowl with plastic wrap or a lid and refrigerate for at least 1 hour to allow the flavors to blend.
3. Serve the tzatziki sauce chilled with a platter of fresh veggies like cherry tomatoes, bell pepper slices, and carrot sticks for dipping.
4. Store any leftover tzatziki sauce in an airtight container in the refrigerator for up to 3 days.

Nutritional Information: Per serving: 95 calories, 6g protein, 8g carbohydrates, 4g fat, 1g fiber, 5mg cholesterol, 190mg sodium, 290mg potassium.

Oven-Roasted Brussels Sprouts

Yield: 4 servings | Prep time: 10 minutes | Cook time: 25 minutes

Ingredients:

- 450 grams Brussels sprouts, trimmed and halved
- 2 tablespoons extra virgin olive oil
- 1/4 teaspoon salt
- 1/4 teaspoon black pepper
- 1/4 teaspoon garlic powder

Directions:

1. Preheat your oven to 220°C (425°F) and line a baking sheet with parchment paper.
2. In a large bowl, toss the trimmed and halved Brussels sprouts with olive oil, salt, black pepper, and garlic powder until they are evenly coated.
3. Spread the Brussels sprouts in a single layer on the prepared baking sheet, making sure they are not overcrowded.
4. Roast the Brussels sprouts in the preheated oven for about 20-25 minutes, stirring once halfway through, until they are golden brown and crispy on the edges.
5. Remove from the oven and serve immediately.

Nutritional Information: Per serving: 89 calories, 3g protein, 11g carbohydrates, 5g fat, 4g fiber, 0mg cholesterol, 158mg sodium, 441mg potassium.

Quinoa and Roasted Vegetable Salad

Yield: 4 servings | Prep time: 15 minutes | Cook time: 30 minutes

Ingredients:

- 150 grams quinoa, rinsed and drained
- 300 millilitres water
- 1 medium courgette, chopped
- 1 medium red bell pepper, chopped
- 1 medium yellow bell pepper, chopped
- 2 tablespoons extra virgin olive oil
- 1/4 teaspoon salt
- 1/4 teaspoon black pepper
- 1 tablespoon fresh lemon juice
- 2 tablespoons fresh parsley, chopped

Directions:

1. Preheat the oven to 220°C (425°F). In a baking tray, combine the chopped courgette and bell peppers with 1 tablespoon of olive oil, salt, and black pepper. Toss until vegetables are evenly coated.
2. Spread the vegetables in an even layer on the baking tray and roast in the preheated oven for about 25-30 minutes, stirring once halfway through, until they are tender and browned at the edges.
3. While the vegetables are roasting, combine the quinoa and water in a medium saucepan. Bring to a boil, then reduce heat to low, cover, and simmer for about 15 minutes until the quinoa is cooked and the water is absorbed. Remove from heat and let it sit covered for 5 minutes, then fluff with a fork.
4. In a large bowl, combine the roasted vegetables, cooked quinoa, lemon juice, parsley, and remaining 1 tablespoon of olive oil. Toss until everything is evenly mixed. Serve immediately or refrigerate for later.

Nutritional Information: Per serving: 193 calories, 6g protein, 29g carbohydrates, 7g fat, 4g fiber, 0mg cholesterol, 152mg sodium, 350mg potassium.

Garlic and Herb Mashed Potatoes

Yield: 4 servings | Prep time: 10 minutes | Cook time: 20 minutes

Ingredients:

- 500 grams potatoes, peeled and chopped into small pieces
- 3 garlic cloves, minced
- 60 millilitres milk (low sodium, low potassium, or suitable alternative)
- 2 tablespoons unsalted butter
- 1 tablespoon fresh parsley, chopped
- 1 tablespoon fresh chives, chopped
- 1/4 teaspoon black pepper

Directions:

1. Place the chopped potatoes in a large pot and cover them with water. Bring to a boil over high heat, then reduce to medium-low and simmer for 10-15 minutes, or until the potatoes are fork-tender.
2. While the potatoes are cooking, in a small saucepan, melt the butter over low heat and add the minced garlic. Cook, stirring frequently, for about 1-2 minutes until the garlic is fragrant but not browned.
3. Drain the cooked potatoes and return them to the pot. Add the milk, butter-garlic mixture, parsley, chives, and black pepper. Mash the potatoes until they reach your desired level of smoothness.
4. Serve hot, garnished with additional herbs if desired.

Nutritional Information: Per serving: 157 calories, 3g protein, 28g carbohydrates, 4g fat, 3g fiber, 11mg cholesterol, 29mg sodium, 532mg potassium.

Avocado and Tomato Salsa

Yield: 4 servings | Prep time: 10 minutes | Cook time: 0 minutes

Ingredients:

- 1 medium avocado, pitted, peeled, and diced (about 150 grams)
- 2 medium tomatoes, deseeded and diced (about 200 grams)
- 1 small red onion, finely chopped (about 50 grams)
- 1 small red chilli, deseeded and finely chopped (optional)
- 2 tablespoons fresh coriander (cilantro), chopped
- 1 tablespoon fresh lime juice (about 15 millilitres)
- 1/4 teaspoon black pepper

Directions:

1. In a medium-sized bowl, combine the diced avocado, tomatoes, chopped red onion, chilli (if using), and fresh coriander.
2. Drizzle the lime juice over the mixture and sprinkle with black pepper.
3. Gently toss the ingredients until well combined. Taste and adjust the seasoning, if needed.
4. Serve immediately as a side dish, topping, or with low-sodium tortilla chips.

Nutritional Information: Per serving: 86 calories, 1g protein, 8g carbohydrates, 6g fat, 4g fiber, 0mg cholesterol, 7mg sodium, 337mg potassium.

Roasted Butternut Squash

Yield: 4 servings | Prep time: 10 minutes | Cook time: 30 minutes

Ingredients:

- 1 medium butternut squash (about 800 grams), peeled, deseeded, and cut into 2cm cubes
- 2 tablespoons olive oil (30 millilitres)
- 1/4 teaspoon black pepper
- 1/4 teaspoon dried thyme
- 1/4 teaspoon dried rosemary

Directions:

1. Preheat your oven to 220°C (425°F).
2. In a large mixing bowl, combine the butternut squash cubes, olive oil, black pepper, thyme, and rosemary. Toss until the squash is well-coated with the oil and spices.
3. Spread the seasoned squash cubes on a baking sheet in a single layer, ensuring they are not overcrowded.
4. Roast in the preheated oven for 25-30 minutes, turning the cubes halfway through the cooking time, until the squash is tender and lightly browned.
5. Remove from the oven and serve hot as a side dish or mixed into a salad.

Nutritional Information: Per serving: 124 calories, 1g protein, 22g carbohydrates, 4g fat, 4g fiber, 0mg cholesterol, 6mg sodium, 582mg potassium.

Lemon and Garlic Green Beans

Yield: 4 servings | Prep time: 5 minutes | Cook time: 10 minutes

Ingredients:

- 400 grams green beans, trimmed
- 2 tablespoons olive oil (30 millilitres)
- 3 cloves garlic, minced
- Zest and juice of 1 lemon
- 1/4 teaspoon black pepper
- 1/4 teaspoon dried basil

Directions:

1. Bring a large pot of water to a boil. Add the green beans and cook for 3-4 minutes, until just tender. Drain and immediately transfer the beans to a bowl of ice water to stop the cooking process. Drain again and set aside.
2. In a large skillet, heat the olive oil over medium heat. Add the garlic and sauté for about 1 minute, until fragrant.
3. Add the green beans to the skillet and toss to coat with the garlic and oil. Cook for 2-3 minutes, until the beans are heated through.
4. Add the lemon zest, lemon juice, black pepper, and dried basil. Toss to combine and cook for an additional 1-2 minutes.
5. Serve hot as a side dish.

Nutritional Information: Per serving: 74 calories, 1.6g protein, 6.4g carbohydrates, 5.3g fat, 2.4g fiber, 0mg cholesterol, 8mg sodium, 194mg potassium.

Baked Zucchini Chips

Yield: 4 servings | Prep time: 10 minutes | Cook time: 20 minutes

Ingredients:

- 2 medium zucchinis (about 400 grams total), sliced into 3 mm thick rounds
- 1 tablespoon olive oil (15 millilitres)
- 1/4 teaspoon salt
- 1/4 teaspoon black pepper
- 1/4 teaspoon garlic powder
- 1/4 teaspoon dried oregano

Directions:

1. Preheat your oven to 220°C (425°F) and line a baking sheet with parchment paper or a silicone baking mat.
2. In a large bowl, toss the zucchini slices with the olive oil, salt, black pepper, garlic powder, and dried oregano.
3. Spread the zucchini slices out on the prepared baking sheet in a single layer, making sure they are not overlapping.
4. Bake in the preheated oven for 20 minutes, turning the zucchini slices over halfway through, until they are golden brown and crispy.
5. Let the zucchini chips cool slightly on the baking sheet before serving. Serve as a snack or side dish.

Nutritional Information: Per serving: 38 calories, 1.1g protein, 2.9g carbohydrates, 2.8g fat, 0.9g fiber, 0mg cholesterol, 149mg sodium, 243mg potassium.

Creamy Garlic Mushrooms

Yield: 4 servings | Prep time: 5 minutes | Cook time: 15 minutes

Ingredients:

- 400 grams of mushrooms, cleaned and sliced
- 2 tablespoons (30 millilitres) of olive oil
- 4 garlic cloves, minced
- 150 millilitres of low-sodium vegetable broth
- 50 millilitres of low-fat cream
- 1/2 teaspoon of dried thyme
- 1/2 teaspoon of dried oregano
- Salt and pepper to taste
- Chopped fresh parsley for garnish (optional)

Directions:

1. In a large skillet, heat the olive oil over medium heat. Add the sliced mushrooms and cook, stirring frequently, for about 5-7 minutes or until the mushrooms are browned and tender.
2. Add the minced garlic to the skillet and cook for an additional 1-2 minutes until fragrant.
3. Pour the vegetable broth into the skillet and bring to a simmer. Let it simmer for 3-4 minutes, allowing the mushrooms to absorb the flavors.
4. Stir in the low-fat cream, thyme, oregano, salt, and pepper. Cook for another 2-3 minutes until the sauce is heated through and slightly thickened.
5. Serve the creamy garlic mushrooms as a side dish, topped with fresh parsley if desired.

Nutritional Information: Per serving: 101 calories, 2.6g protein, 5.2g carbohydrates, 8.4g fat, 1.4g fiber, 3mg cholesterol, 89mg sodium, 399mg potassium.

Honey Glazed Carrots

Yield: 4 servings | Prep time: 10 minutes | Cook time: 15 minutes

Ingredients:

- 500 grams of carrots, peeled and sliced into 1 cm thick rounds
- 2 tablespoons (30 millilitres) of olive oil
- 2 tablespoons (30 millilitres) of honey
- 1/2 teaspoon of dried thyme
- 1/2 teaspoon of dried rosemary
- Salt and pepper to taste
- Chopped fresh parsley for garnish (optional)

Directions:

1. In a large skillet, heat the olive oil over medium heat. Add the sliced carrots and cook, stirring occasionally, for about 5-7 minutes or until the carrots are beginning to soften.
2. In a small bowl, whisk together the honey, thyme, and rosemary. Pour this mixture over the carrots in the skillet.
3. Continue cooking the carrots, stirring frequently, for an additional 5-7 minutes or until the carrots are tender and glazed with the honey mixture.
4. Season with salt and pepper to taste.
5. Serve the honey glazed carrots as a side dish, topped with fresh parsley if desired.

Nutritional Information: Per serving: 123 calories, 1g protein, 20g carbohydrates, 5g fat, 3g fiber, 0mg cholesterol, 89mg sodium, 369mg potassium.

Oven-Baked Asparagus with Parmesan

Yield: 4 servings | Prep time: 10 minutes | Cook time: 10 minutes

Ingredients:

- 500 grams of fresh asparagus, ends trimmed
- 2 tablespoons (30 millilitres) of olive oil
- 30 grams of grated Parmesan cheese
- 1/2 teaspoon of garlic powder
- Salt and pepper to taste
- Chopped fresh parsley for garnish (optional)

Directions:

1. Preheat your oven to 220 degrees Celsius (425 degrees Fahrenheit).
2. Place the trimmed asparagus in a baking dish and drizzle with olive oil. Toss the asparagus to coat with the oil.
3. Sprinkle the asparagus with the garlic powder, salt, and pepper. Toss again to evenly coat.
4. Sprinkle the grated Parmesan cheese over the asparagus.
5. Bake in the preheated oven for about 10 minutes, or until the asparagus is tender and the cheese is melted and lightly browned.
6. Garnish with fresh parsley if desired, and serve immediately.

Nutritional Information: Per serving: 114 calories, 4g protein, 6g carbohydrates, 9g fat, 3g fiber, 5mg cholesterol, 147mg sodium, 230mg potassium.

Spinach and Artichoke Dip

Yield: 4 servings | Prep time: 10 minutes | Cook time: 20 minutes

Ingredients:

- 200 grams of fresh spinach, chopped
- 1 can (about 400 grams) of artichoke hearts, drained and chopped
- 120 grams of cream cheese, softened
- 100 grams of plain Greek yogurt
- 50 grams of grated Parmesan cheese
- 2 cloves garlic, minced
- 1/4 teaspoon of black pepper
- 1/4 teaspoon of salt
- 1 tablespoon (15 millilitres) of olive oil

Directions:

1. Preheat your oven to 180 degrees Celsius (350 degrees Fahrenheit).
2. In a medium-sized bowl, mix together the cream cheese, Greek yogurt, Parmesan cheese, garlic, black pepper, and salt until well combined.
3. Fold in the chopped spinach and artichoke hearts.
4. Transfer the mixture to an oven-safe dish, and drizzle with olive oil.
5. Bake in the preheated oven for about 20 minutes, or until the dip is heated through and the top is lightly browned.
6. Serve warm with cut-up vegetables, whole-grain crackers, or pita bread.

Nutritional Information: Per serving: 214 calories, 9g protein, 8g carbohydrates, 17g fat, 3g fiber, 47mg cholesterol, 486mg sodium, 215mg potassium.

Tomato and Basil Salad

Yield: 4 servings | Prep time: 10 minutes | Cook time: 0 minutes

Ingredients:

- 500 grams of cherry tomatoes, halved
- 50 grams of fresh basil leaves, torn into small pieces
- 50 grams of red onion, thinly sliced
- 1 clove garlic, minced
- 1 tablespoon (15 millilitres) of olive oil
- 2 tablespoons (30 millilitres) of balsamic vinegar
- Salt and pepper to taste

Directions:

1. In a large bowl, combine the halved cherry tomatoes, torn basil leaves, and sliced red onion.
2. In a small bowl, whisk together the olive oil, balsamic vinegar, minced garlic, salt, and pepper. Adjust the seasoning to taste.
3. Pour the dressing over the tomato mixture and gently toss until the ingredients are evenly coated.
4. Serve immediately or refrigerate for later use. The salad tastes best when served chilled and consumed within a day.

Nutritional Information: Per serving: 62 calories, 1g protein, 6g carbohydrates, 4g fat, 1g fiber, 0mg cholesterol, 6mg sodium, 210mg potassium.

Garlic and Herb Roasted Potatoes

Yield: 4 servings | Prep time: 10 minutes | Cook time: 35 minutes

Ingredients:

- 600 grams of baby potatoes, halved
- 2 tablespoons (30 millilitres) of olive oil
- 4 cloves of garlic, minced
- 2 teaspoons (10 grams) of mixed dried herbs (thyme, rosemary, oregano)
- Salt and pepper to taste
- Fresh parsley, chopped for garnish

Directions:

1. Preheat the oven to 220°C (425°F). Line a baking sheet with parchment paper or a silicone baking mat.
2. In a large bowl, toss the halved baby potatoes with the olive oil, minced garlic, dried herbs, salt, and pepper. Make sure the potatoes are evenly coated.
3. Spread the potatoes in a single layer on the prepared baking sheet, ensuring that they are not overcrowded.
4. Roast the potatoes in the preheated oven for about 30-35 minutes, or until they are golden brown and crispy on the outside, and tender on the inside. Stir or shake the pan halfway through cooking to ensure even browning.
5. Remove the potatoes from the oven and transfer them to a serving dish. Sprinkle with chopped fresh parsley and serve immediately.

Nutritional Information: Per serving: 191 calories, 3g protein, 29g carbohydrates, 7g fat, 3g fiber, 0mg cholesterol, 9mg sodium, 720mg potassium.

Vegetarian and Vegan Choices

Eggplant Parmesan

Yield: 4 servings | Prep time: 15 minutes | Cook time: 45 minutes

Ingredients:

- 2 medium-sized eggplants (about 700 grams), sliced into 1 cm thick rounds
- 2 tablespoons (30 millilitres) olive oil
- 100 grams plain breadcrumbs
- 1 teaspoon (5 grams) dried oregano
- 1 teaspoon (5 grams) dried basil
- Salt and pepper to taste
- 150 grams low-sodium, low-potassium marinara sauce
- 100 grams mozzarella cheese, grated
- 30 grams Parmesan cheese, grated
- Fresh basil leaves, for garnish

Directions:

1. Preheat the oven to 190°C (375°F). Line a baking sheet with parchment paper or a silicone baking mat.
2. In a shallow dish, combine the breadcrumbs, oregano, basil, salt, and pepper. Brush each slice of eggplant with olive oil on both sides, then dip it into the breadcrumb mixture, pressing to coat both sides.
3. Arrange the coated eggplant slices in a single layer on the prepared baking sheet. Bake for 25-30 minutes, flipping the slices halfway through, until they are golden brown and crispy.
4. In a baking dish, spread a thin layer of marinara sauce. Layer half of the baked eggplant slices on top, followed by half of the mozzarella and half of the Parmesan cheese. Repeat the layers with the remaining ingredients.
5. Bake for 15 minutes, or until the cheese is melted and bubbly.
6. Garnish with fresh basil leaves before serving.

Nutritional Information: Per serving: 297 calories, 11g protein, 32g carbohydrates, 15g fat, 9g fiber, 21mg cholesterol, 307mg sodium, 491mg potassium.

Vegan Sweet Potato and Black Bean Tacos

Yield: 4 servings | Prep time: 15 minutes | Cook time: 35 minutes

Ingredients:

- 2 large sweet potatoes (about 600 grams), peeled and diced into small cubes
- 2 tablespoons (30 millilitres) olive oil
- 1 teaspoon (5 millilitres) cumin
- 1 teaspoon (5 millilitres) smoked paprika
- Salt and pepper, to taste
- 1 can (400 grams) low-sodium black beans, drained and rinsed
- 8 small corn tortillas
- 1 small red onion (about 100 grams), finely chopped
- 1 lime, juiced (about 30 millilitres)
- 2 tablespoons (30 millilitres) fresh coriander, chopped
- 1 avocado (about 150 grams), sliced

Directions:

1. Preheat the oven to 200°C (400°F). Place the diced sweet potatoes on a baking sheet. Drizzle with 1 tablespoon of olive oil and sprinkle with cumin, smoked paprika, salt, and pepper. Toss to coat. Roast for 25-30 minutes or until the sweet potatoes are tender and lightly browned.
2. In a large skillet, heat the remaining 1 tablespoon of olive oil over medium heat. Add the black beans and cook for 5 minutes until heated through. Season with salt and pepper.
3. In a small bowl, mix together the chopped red onion, lime juice, and fresh coriander. Season with salt and pepper.
4. Assemble the tacos: Place a few spoonfuls of the roasted sweet potatoes and black beans on each tortilla. Top with the red onion and coriander mixture and a few slices of avocado. Fold the tortilla in half to serve.

Nutritional Information: Per serving: 370 calories, 11g protein, 60g carbohydrates, 11g fat, 13g fiber, 0mg cholesterol, 320mg sodium, 980mg potassium.

Vegetarian Chili with Kidney Beans

Yield: 4 servings | Prep time: 10 minutes | Cook time: 30 minutes

Ingredients:

- 1 tablespoon (15 millilitres) olive oil
- 1 onion, diced (about 150 grams)
- 2 cloves garlic, minced
- 1 bell pepper, diced (about 150 grams)
- 2 carrots, diced (about 120 grams)
- 1 teaspoon (5 millilitres) chili powder
- 1 teaspoon (5 millilitres) ground cumin
- 1 teaspoon (5 millilitres) paprika
- 400 grams canned diced tomatoes (low-sodium)
- 400 grams canned kidney beans, drained and rinsed
- 200 millilitres vegetable stock (low-sodium)
- Salt to taste
- Fresh coriander leaves for garnish

Directions:

1. In a large saucepan, heat the olive oil over medium heat. Add the diced onion, garlic, bell pepper, and carrots. Cook for 5-7 minutes, until the vegetables are softened.
2. Stir in the chili powder, ground cumin, and paprika. Cook for 1-2 minutes, until the spices are fragrant.
3. Add the diced tomatoes, kidney beans, and vegetable stock to the saucepan. Stir to combine.
4. Bring the mixture to a simmer and let it cook for 20-25 minutes, stirring occasionally, until the chili has thickened and the flavors have melded together.
5. Season with salt to taste and garnish with fresh coriander leaves before serving.

Nutritional Information: Per serving: 235 calories, 10g protein, 42g carbohydrates, 4g fat, 12g fiber, 0mg cholesterol, 330mg sodium, 840mg potassium.

Vegan Lentil and Vegetable Stew

Yield: 4 servings | Prep time: 20 minutes | Cook time: 40 minutes

Ingredients:

- 150 grams green lentils, rinsed and drained
- 1 tablespoon (15 millilitres) olive oil
- 1 medium onion, chopped
- 2 cloves garlic, minced
- 2 medium carrots, diced
- 1 medium zucchini, diced
- 400 grams tinned chopped tomatoes (low sodium)
- 1 litre vegetable stock (low sodium)
- 1 teaspoon (5 grams) dried thyme
- 1/2 teaspoon (2.5 grams) dried rosemary
- 1/4 teaspoon (1 gram) black pepper
- 1 handful fresh parsley, chopped (for garnish)

Directions:

1. In a large pot, heat olive oil over medium heat. Add onions and garlic, and sauté until translucent, about 5 minutes.
2. Add carrots and zucchini to the pot and cook for an additional 5 minutes, stirring occasionally.
3. Stir in the lentils, tinned tomatoes, vegetable stock, thyme, rosemary, and black pepper. Bring to a boil.
4. Once boiling, reduce heat to low and let simmer for about 30 minutes, or until lentils are tender and fully cooked.
5. Serve the stew in bowls, garnished with fresh parsley.

Nutritional Information: Per serving: 210 calories, 12g protein, 35g carbohydrates, 3g fat, 14g fiber, 0mg cholesterol, 200mg sodium, 650mg potassium.

Mushroom Stroganoff

Yield: 4 servings | Prep time: 10 minutes | Cook time: 20 minutes

Ingredients:

- 400 grams mushrooms, sliced
- 1 onion, diced (about 150 grams)
- 2 cloves garlic, minced
- 1 tablespoon (15 millilitres) olive oil
- 1 teaspoon (5 millilitres) paprika
- 200 millilitres low-sodium vegetable broth
- 100 millilitres sour cream (low-fat)
- 2 tablespoons (30 millilitres) fresh parsley, chopped
- 1 teaspoon (5 millilitres) Dijon mustard
- Salt and pepper, to taste

Directions:

1. Heat olive oil in a large skillet over medium heat. Add the diced onions and garlic. Cook for 2-3 minutes until softened.
2. Add the sliced mushrooms to the skillet. Cook for 8-10 minutes until the mushrooms have browned and released their juices.
3. Sprinkle the paprika over the mushrooms. Stir to combine.
4. Add the vegetable broth and Dijon mustard to the skillet. Stir well to combine. Simmer for 5-6 minutes until the sauce has thickened.
5. Remove from heat and stir in the sour cream and chopped parsley. Season with salt and pepper to taste.
6. Serve the mushroom stroganoff over rice, pasta, or mashed potatoes, as desired.

Nutritional Information: Per serving: 120 calories, 4g protein, 10g carbohydrates, 8g fat, 2g fiber, 10mg cholesterol, 100mg sodium, 400mg potassium.

Vegetarian Stuffed Portobello Mushrooms

Yield: 4 servings | Prep time: 15 minutes | Cook time: 25 minutes

Ingredients:

- 4 large portobello mushrooms, stems removed and gills scraped out
- 1 tablespoon (15 millilitres) olive oil
- 1 small onion, finely chopped
- 2 cloves garlic, minced
- 150 grams cooked quinoa
- 1 medium tomato, chopped
- 60 grams feta cheese, crumbled
- 1 tablespoon (15 grams) fresh basil, chopped
- 1/4 teaspoon (1.5 grams) salt
- 1/4 teaspoon (0.5 grams) black pepper
- 1 tablespoon (15 millilitres) balsamic glaze (optional)

Directions:

1. Preheat your oven to 190°C (375°F). Line a baking sheet with parchment paper.
2. Place the cleaned portobello mushrooms on the baking sheet, cap side down.
3. In a skillet, heat the olive oil over medium heat. Add the onion and garlic, and sauté until soft, about 5 minutes.
4. Remove the skillet from heat and stir in the cooked quinoa, chopped tomato, crumbled feta cheese, and chopped basil. Season with salt and pepper.
5. Spoon the quinoa mixture into each portobello mushroom cap, pressing down slightly to pack the filling.
6. Bake the stuffed mushrooms in the preheated oven for 15-20 minutes, or until the mushrooms are tender and the filling is heated through.
7. (Optional) Drizzle the stuffed mushrooms with balsamic glaze before serving.

Nutritional Information: Per serving: 165 calories, 6g protein, 21g carbohydrates, 7g fat, 4g fiber, 15mg cholesterol, 355mg sodium, 440mg potassium.

Vegetarian Quiche with Spinach and Cheese

Yield: 6 servings | Prep time: 20 minutes | Cook time: 35 minutes

Ingredients:

- 1 pre-made pie crust (about 200 grams)
- 200 grams fresh spinach leaves, washed and drained
- 1 medium onion, chopped
- 2 cloves garlic, minced
- 4 large eggs
- 150 millilitres whole milk
- 100 grams grated cheddar cheese
- 1/2 teaspoon (2.5 grams) salt
- 1/4 teaspoon (1 gram) black pepper
- 1/4 teaspoon (1 gram) ground nutmeg
- 1 tablespoon (15 millilitres) vegetable oil

Directions:

1. Preheat your oven to 190°C (375°F). Place the pie crust in a 9-inch (23 cm) pie dish and bake for 10 minutes. Remove from the oven and set aside.
2. In a large skillet, heat the vegetable oil over medium heat. Add the onion and garlic, and sauté for 3-4 minutes until softened. Add the spinach and cook for 2-3 minutes until wilted. Remove from heat and let it cool.
3. In a medium bowl, whisk together the eggs, milk, salt, pepper, and nutmeg. Stir in the grated cheese.
4. Spread the spinach mixture evenly over the pre-baked pie crust. Pour the egg mixture over the spinach.
5. Bake the quiche for 30-35 minutes, or until the centre is set and the top is golden brown. Let it cool for a few minutes before slicing and serving.

Nutritional Information: Per serving: 250 calories, 11g protein, 18g carbohydrates, 15g fat, 2g fiber, 160mg cholesterol, 450mg sodium, 300mg potassium.

Eggplant and Tomato Caponata

Yield: 4 servings | Prep time: 15 minutes | Cook time: 30 minutes

Ingredients:

- 1 large eggplant (about 450 grams), diced into 2 cm cubes
- 3 tablespoons (45 millilitres) olive oil
- 1 medium onion (about 150 grams), chopped
- 3 cloves garlic (about 9 grams), minced
- 400 grams canned tomatoes, drained and chopped
- 1 tablespoon (15 millilitres) red wine vinegar
- 1 teaspoon (5 grams) capers, rinsed and drained
- 1 tablespoon (15 grams) raisins or sultanas
- 1 teaspoon (5 grams) dried oregano
- 1/2 teaspoon (2 grams) crushed red pepper flakes (optional)
- Fresh basil leaves, for garnish
- Salt and black pepper to taste

Directions:

1. Preheat the oven to 200°C (180°C for fan ovens). Place the diced eggplant on a baking sheet, toss with 2 tablespoons of olive oil, and season with a pinch of salt and black pepper. Roast for 20-25 minutes, or until the eggplant is soft and golden.
2. In a large skillet, heat 1 tablespoon of olive oil over medium heat. Add the chopped onion and sauté for 3-4 minutes, or until softened. Add the minced garlic and sauté for another minute.
3. Add the roasted eggplant, chopped tomatoes, red wine vinegar, capers, raisins or sultanas, dried oregano, and crushed red pepper flakes (if using). Stir to combine and simmer for 5 minutes, or until heated through.
4. Season with salt and black pepper to taste. Garnish with fresh basil leaves before serving.

Nutritional Information: Per serving: 160 calories, 2g protein, 19g carbohydrates, 9g fat, 6g fiber, 0mg cholesterol, 260mg sodium, 420mg potassium.

Vegetarian Lasagna with Spinach

Yield: 6 servings | Prep time: 15 minutes | Cook time: 45 minutes

Ingredients:

- 12 no-boil lasagna sheets (about 250 grams)
- 2 tablespoons (30 millilitres) olive oil
- 1 onion (about 150 grams), chopped
- 3 cloves garlic (about 9 grams), minced
- 200 grams fresh spinach, washed and roughly chopped
- 1 can (400 grams) low-sodium diced tomatoes
- 250 grams ricotta cheese
- 100 grams low-fat mozzarella cheese, shredded
- 50 grams parmesan cheese, grated
- 1 teaspoon (5 millilitres) dried basil
- 1 teaspoon (5 millilitres) dried oregano
- Salt and pepper, to taste

Directions:

1. Preheat your oven to 180°C (350°F). In a large skillet, heat olive oil over medium heat. Add onion and garlic, and cook until softened, about 5 minutes. Add spinach and cook until wilted, about 3 minutes. Add tomatoes, basil, oregano, salt, and pepper. Simmer for 10 minutes.
2. In a bowl, mix together ricotta cheese, half of the mozzarella, half of the parmesan, salt, and pepper.
3. Spread a small amount of the tomato and spinach sauce on the bottom of a baking dish. Place 3 lasagna sheets on top. Spread half of the ricotta mixture over the noodles, followed by a third of the sauce. Repeat layers ending with lasagna sheets. Top with remaining sauce, mozzarella, and parmesan.
4. Cover with foil and bake for 30 minutes. Remove foil and bake for an additional 15 minutes, or until the top is golden and bubbly.

Nutritional Information: Per serving: 325 calories, 17g protein, 40g carbohydrates, 12g fat, 4g fiber, 25mg cholesterol, 340mg sodium, 380mg potassium.

Vegan Lentil Shepherd's Pie

Yield: 4 servings | Prep time: 20 minutes | Cook time: 45 minutes

Ingredients:

- 150 grams dried green lentils, rinsed and drained
- 500 millilitres water
- 2 tablespoons (30 millilitres) olive oil
- 1 medium onion (about 150 grams), finely chopped
- 2 cloves garlic, minced
- 2 medium carrots (about 120 grams), diced
- 2 stalks celery (about 100 grams), diced
- 2 tablespoons (30 grams) tomato paste
- 1 teaspoon (5 grams) dried thyme
- 1 teaspoon (5 grams) dried rosemary
- Salt and pepper to taste
- 500 grams cauliflower florets
- 1 tablespoon (15 millilitres) olive oil
- 2 tablespoons (30 millilitres) unsweetened almond milk

Directions:

1. In a medium saucepan, bring the water to a boil. Add the lentils and cook for 25 minutes, or until tender but not mushy. Drain and set aside.
2. Preheat the oven to 190°C (375°F).
3. In a large skillet, heat the olive oil over medium heat. Add the onion, garlic, carrots, and celery, and cook for 5-7 minutes, or until the vegetables are softened. Stir in the tomato paste, thyme, rosemary, salt, and pepper. Add the cooked lentils and stir to combine.
4. Transfer the lentil mixture to a baking dish, spreading it out evenly.
5. In a medium saucepan, steam the cauliflower until tender. Mash the cauliflower with the olive oil and almond milk until smooth. Season with salt and pepper to taste.
6. Spread the mashed cauliflower over the lentil mixture in the baking dish. Bake for 20 minutes, or until the top is lightly browned.

Nutritional Information: Per serving: 280 calories, 13g protein, 38g carbohydrates, 9g fat, 12g fiber, 0mg cholesterol, 203mg sodium, 809mg potassium.

Stuffed Acorn Squash with Quinoa

Yield: 4 servings | Prep time: 15 minutes | Cook time: 50 minutes

Ingredients:

- 2 medium acorn squashes (about 1.2 kg total)
- 2 tablespoons (30 millilitres) olive oil, divided
- Salt and pepper to taste
- 120 grams quinoa, rinsed and drained
- 240 millilitres water
- 1 medium onion (about 150 grams), finely chopped
- 2 cloves garlic, minced
- 100 grams cherry tomatoes, halved
- 60 grams baby spinach
- 30 grams pecans, chopped
- 30 grams dried cranberries

Directions:

1. Preheat the oven to 200°C (400°F). Cut the acorn squashes in half lengthwise and scoop out the seeds. Brush the cut sides with 1 tablespoon of olive oil and season with salt and pepper. Place the squash halves cut-side down on a baking sheet and roast for 30 minutes, or until tender.
2. In a medium saucepan, combine the quinoa and water. Bring to a boil, then reduce the heat to low and cover. Simmer for 15 minutes, or until the quinoa is cooked and the water is absorbed. Fluff with a fork and set aside.
3. In a large skillet, heat the remaining tablespoon of olive oil over medium heat. Add the onion and garlic and cook for 5-7 minutes, or until the onion is translucent. Add the cherry tomatoes and cook for an additional 2-3 minutes, or until the tomatoes are softened.
4. Stir the cooked quinoa, spinach, pecans, and cranberries into the skillet. Season with salt and pepper to taste.
5. Divide the quinoa mixture among the roasted acorn squash halves. Serve warm.

Nutritional Information: Per serving: 324 calories, 8g protein, 58g carbohydrates, 9g fat, 9g fiber, 0mg cholesterol, 57mg sodium, 894mg potassium.

Spinach and Ricotta Stuffed Shells

Yield: 4 servings | Prep time: 30 minutes | Cook time: 35 minutes

Ingredients:

- 16 large pasta shells (about 160 grams)
- 200 grams fresh spinach
- 250 grams ricotta cheese
- 1 large egg (about 60 grams)
- 50 grams grated Parmesan cheese
- 1 clove garlic, minced
- 1/2 teaspoon (2.5 millilitres) dried basil
- 1/2 teaspoon (2.5 millilitres) dried oregano
- Salt and pepper to taste
- 250 millilitres low-sodium marinara sauce
- 50 grams shredded mozzarella cheese
- Fresh basil leaves for garnish

Directions:

1. Preheat the oven to 180°C (350°F). Cook the pasta shells according to the package instructions until al dente. Drain and set aside.
2. In a large skillet, wilt the spinach over medium heat, about 3-4 minutes. Remove from heat and let it cool slightly. Squeeze out any excess water and chop the spinach finely.
3. In a large mixing bowl, combine the chopped spinach, ricotta cheese, egg, Parmesan cheese, garlic, dried basil, dried oregano, salt, and pepper. Mix well to combine.
4. Spread a thin layer of marinara sauce at the bottom of a baking dish. Stuff each pasta shell with the spinach and ricotta mixture and place them in the baking dish.
5. Pour the remaining marinara sauce over the stuffed shells and sprinkle with shredded mozzarella cheese.
6. Cover the baking dish with foil and bake for 25 minutes. Remove the foil and bake for an additional 10 minutes, or until the cheese is melted and bubbly.
7. Garnish with fresh basil leaves before serving.

Nutritional Information: Per serving: 340 calories, 19g protein, 34g carbohydrates, 15g fat, 3g fiber, 90mg cholesterol, 470mg sodium, 640mg potassium.

Vegan Chickpea Curry

Yield: 4 servings | Prep time: 10 minutes | Cook time: 25 minutes

Ingredients:

- 1 tablespoon (15 millilitres) olive oil
- 1 onion, diced (about 150 grams)
- 2 cloves garlic, minced
- 1 tablespoon (15 millilitres) curry powder
- 1 teaspoon (5 millilitres) ground cumin
- 1 teaspoon (5 millilitres) ground turmeric
- 1 teaspoon (5 millilitres) ground coriander
- 1/2 teaspoon (2.5 millilitres) ground paprika
- 1/2 teaspoon (2.5 millilitres) chili powder (optional)
- 400 grams canned chickpeas, drained and rinsed
- 400 millilitres canned diced tomatoes (low-sodium)
- 200 millilitres coconut milk (light)
- Salt to taste
- Fresh coriander leaves for garnish

Directions:

1. In a large saucepan, heat the olive oil over medium heat. Add the diced onion and cook for 3-4 minutes, until softened. Add the minced garlic and cook for an additional minute.
2. Stir in the curry powder, ground cumin, ground turmeric, ground coriander, ground paprika, and chili powder (if using). Cook for 1-2 minutes, stirring constantly, until the spices are fragrant.
3. Add the drained chickpeas, diced tomatoes, and coconut milk to the saucepan. Stir to combine.
4. Bring the mixture to a simmer and let it cook for 15-20 minutes, stirring occasionally, until the curry has thickened and the flavors have melded together.
5. Season with salt to taste and garnish with fresh coriander leaves before serving.

Nutritional Information: Per serving: 295 calories, 10g protein, 37g carbohydrates, 13g fat, 9g fiber, 0mg cholesterol, 240mg sodium, 620mg potassium.

Vegan Thai Green Curry

Yield: 4 servings | Prep time: 15 minutes | Cook time: 25 minutes

Ingredients:

- 1 tablespoon (15 millilitres) coconut oil
- 1 onion (about 150 grams), chopped
- 3 cloves garlic (about 9 grams), minced
- 2 tablespoons (30 millilitres) low-sodium soy sauce
- 2 tablespoons (30 millilitres) vegan Thai green curry paste
- 1 can (400 millilitres) light coconut milk
- 200 grams firm tofu, cubed
- 1 medium red bell pepper (about 150 grams), sliced
- 1 medium green bell pepper (about 150 grams), sliced
- 1 medium carrot (about 60 grams), sliced
- 150 grams baby corn, chopped
- 1 tablespoon (15 millilitres) lime juice
- Fresh basil and coriander leaves, for garnish

Directions:

1. Heat the coconut oil in a large saucepan over medium heat. Add the chopped onion and sauté for 3-4 minutes, or until softened. Add the minced garlic and sauté for another minute.
2. Stir in the low-sodium soy sauce and vegan Thai green curry paste. Cook for 2 minutes, stirring frequently.
3. Pour in the light coconut milk, bring the mixture to a simmer, and cook for 10 minutes, stirring occasionally.
4. Add the tofu, red and green bell peppers, carrot, and baby corn. Simmer for 10 minutes, or until the vegetables are tender.
5. Stir in the lime juice. Garnish with fresh basil and coriander leaves before serving.

Nutritional Information: Per serving: 210 calories, 8g protein, 18g carbohydrates, 12g fat, 3g fiber, 0mg cholesterol, 480mg sodium, 400mg potassium.

Vegan Sushi Rolls with Avocado

Yield: 4 servings | Prep time: 30 minutes | Cook time: 25 minutes

Ingredients:

- 200 grams sushi rice
- 375 millilitres water
- 3 tablespoons (45 millilitres) rice vinegar
- 1 tablespoon (15 grams) sugar
- 1/2 teaspoon (3 grams) salt
- 4 nori sheets (seaweed)
- 1 ripe avocado, sliced
- 1 small cucumber, julienned
- 1 small red bell pepper, julienned
- 1 small carrot, julienned
- Soy sauce, for dipping (low sodium)

Directions:

1. Rinse the sushi rice under cold water until the water runs clear. Add the rice and water to a saucepan and bring to a boil. Reduce heat to low, cover, and simmer for 20 minutes. Remove from heat and let it sit for 5 minutes.
2. While the rice is cooking, combine the rice vinegar, sugar, and salt in a small saucepan. Heat over low heat, stirring until the sugar and salt dissolve. Cool to room temperature.
3. Transfer the cooked rice to a large bowl and gently fold in the vinegar mixture until the rice is coated. Let the rice cool to room temperature.
4. Lay a nori sheet on a bamboo sushi rolling mat. Wet your fingers and spread a layer of rice on the nori, leaving about 2 cm of nori exposed at the top. Arrange a few slices of avocado and julienned vegetables on the rice.
5. Roll the sushi tightly using the bamboo mat, pressing firmly as you roll. Repeat with the remaining nori sheets, rice, and fillings.
6. Slice the sushi rolls into bite-sized pieces using a sharp, wet knife. Serve with low-sodium soy sauce for dipping.

Nutritional Information: Per serving: 235 calories, 5g protein, 49g carbohydrates, 5g fat, 5g fiber, 0mg cholesterol, 295mg sodium, 375mg potassium.

Vegetarian Greek Salad with Tofu Feta

Yield: 4 servings | Prep time: 15 minutes | Cook time: 0 minutes

Ingredients:

- 200 grams tofu, pressed and cubed
- 2 tablespoons (30 millilitres) lemon juice
- 2 tablespoons (30 millilitres) apple cider vinegar
- 1 tablespoon (15 millilitres) olive oil
- 1 teaspoon (5 grams) dried oregano
- 1/2 teaspoon (2.5 grams) garlic powder
- 1/4 teaspoon (1 gram) black pepper
- 4 medium tomatoes, diced
- 1 medium cucumber, diced
- 1 small red onion, thinly sliced
- 50 grams Kalamata olives, pitted and halved
- 2 tablespoons (30 millilitres) balsamic vinegar
- 1 tablespoon (15 millilitres) extra-virgin olive oil
- 1/4 teaspoon (1 gram) dried oregano
- Fresh basil leaves, for garnish

Directions:

1. In a bowl, combine tofu, lemon juice, apple cider vinegar, olive oil, oregano, garlic powder, and black pepper. Mix well and let marinate for at least 30 minutes in the refrigerator.
2. In a large salad bowl, combine tomatoes, cucumber, red onion, and olives.
3. In a small bowl, whisk together balsamic vinegar, extra-virgin olive oil, and dried oregano. Pour dressing over the vegetables and toss to coat.
4. Add marinated tofu feta to the salad and gently toss to combine.
5. Garnish with fresh basil leaves and serve immediately.

Nutritional Information: Per serving: 190 calories, 9g protein, 14g carbohydrates, 12g fat, 3g fiber, 0mg cholesterol, 200mg sodium, 380mg potassium.

Vegan Cauliflower and Potato Curry

Yield: 4 servings | Prep time: 15 minutes | Cook time: 30 minutes

Ingredients:

- 1 large head of cauliflower, cut into florets (about 500 grams)
- 2 medium potatoes, peeled and diced (about 300 grams)
- 1 large onion, chopped
- 3 cloves garlic, minced
- 1 tablespoon (15 millilitres) vegetable oil
- 1 tablespoon (15 grams) curry powder
- 1 teaspoon (5 grams) ground cumin
- 1 teaspoon (5 grams) ground coriander
- 1/2 teaspoon (2.5 grams) turmeric
- 1/4 teaspoon (1 gram) cayenne pepper (optional, adjust to taste)
- 400 millilitres canned chopped tomatoes
- 200 millilitres water
- Salt to taste (if needed)
- Fresh coriander leaves, for garnish

Directions:

1. Heat the vegetable oil in a large pan over medium heat. Add the onion and garlic and sauté for 3-4 minutes until soft.
2. Add the curry powder, cumin, coriander, turmeric, and cayenne pepper (if using). Cook for 1-2 minutes, stirring constantly, until fragrant.
3. Add the cauliflower, potatoes, canned tomatoes, and water to the pan. Stir well to coat the vegetables with the spices and bring the mixture to a simmer.
4. Cover and cook for 20-25 minutes, stirring occasionally, until the cauliflower and potatoes are tender.
5. Taste and adjust seasoning with salt if needed. Serve hot, garnished with fresh coriander leaves.

Nutritional Information: Per serving: 160 calories, 5g protein, 30g carbohydrates, 3g fat, 7g fiber, 0mg cholesterol, 100mg sodium, 800mg potassium.

Vegan Pad Thai with Tofu

Yield: 4 servings | Prep time: 15 minutes | Cook time: 15 minutes

Ingredients:

- 200 grams rice noodles
- 200 grams firm tofu, drained and cubed
- 2 tablespoons (30 millilitres) vegetable oil
- 2 cloves garlic, minced
- 100 grams carrots, julienned
- 100 grams bell peppers, thinly sliced
- 4 spring onions, sliced
- 100 grams bean sprouts

For the sauce:

- 3 tablespoons (45 millilitres) soy sauce
- 2 tablespoons (30 millilitres) lime juice
- 1 tablespoon (15 millilitres) brown sugar
- 1 tablespoon (15 millilitres) water
- 1/4 teaspoon (1 gram) crushed red pepper flakes (optional)
- Garnish:
- Fresh cilantro, chopped
- Crushed peanuts
- Lime wedges

Directions:

1. Cook the rice noodles according to package instructions, then drain and set aside.
2. In a small bowl, whisk together the sauce ingredients until well combined. Set aside.
3. Heat 1 tablespoon of oil in a large non-stick pan over medium-high heat. Add the tofu and cook, turning occasionally, until all sides are golden brown. Remove the tofu from the pan and set aside.
4. In the same pan, add the remaining tablespoon of oil and sauté the garlic for about 30 seconds. Add the carrots and bell peppers, and cook for 3-4 minutes until slightly softened. Add the spring onions and bean sprouts and stir-fry for another 1-2 minutes.
5. Add the cooked noodles, tofu, and sauce to the pan. Toss everything together until well combined and heated through.
6. Serve the Pad Thai in bowls, garnished with fresh cilantro, crushed peanuts, and lime wedges.

Nutritional Information: Per serving: 280 calories, 11g protein, 40g carbohydrates, 8g fat, 3g fiber, 0mg cholesterol, 600mg sodium, 350mg potassium.

Vegetarian Spring Rolls with Peanut Sauce

Yield: 4 servings | Prep time: 20 minutes | Cook time: 0 minutes

Ingredients:

For the spring rolls:

- 8 rice paper wrappers (about 22cm diameter)
- 100 grams vermicelli noodles, cooked according to package instructions
- 1 carrot, julienned
- 1 cucumber, julienned
- 4 spring onions, thinly sliced
- 8 lettuce leaves
- Fresh coriander leaves
- Fresh mint leaves

For the peanut sauce:

- 2 tablespoons (30 millilitres) smooth peanut butter
- 2 tablespoons (30 millilitres) soy sauce
- 1 tablespoon (15 millilitres) rice vinegar
- 1 tablespoon (15 millilitres) lime juice
- 1 teaspoon (5 millilitres) sesame oil
- 1 teaspoon (5 millilitres) maple syrup
- 1 small clove garlic, minced
- 1/4 teaspoon (1 gram) crushed red pepper flakes (optional)

Directions:

1. To prepare the peanut sauce, whisk together all the sauce ingredients in a small bowl until well combined. Set aside.
2. Dip a rice paper wrapper into a shallow dish of warm water for a few seconds until softened. Place the wrapper on a clean, damp kitchen towel.
3. Layer a small amount of vermicelli noodles, carrot, cucumber, spring onions, lettuce, coriander, and mint on the lower third of the rice paper wrapper, leaving a border around the edges.
4. Fold the bottom edge of the wrapper over the filling, then fold in the sides and roll it up tightly like a burrito.
5. Repeat with the remaining wrappers and filling.
6. Serve the spring rolls with the peanut sauce on the side for dipping.

Nutritional Information: Per serving: 210 calories, 6g protein, 35g carbohydrates, 6g fat, 2g fiber, 0mg cholesterol, 500mg sodium, 400mg potassium.

Desserts and Sweet Treats

Baked Pears with Cinnamon

Yield: 4 servings | Prep time: 10 minutes | Cook time: 25 minutes

Ingredients:

- 4 ripe pears (preferably Bartlett or Conference), halved and cored
- 2 tablespoons (30 millilitres) maple syrup
- 1 teaspoon (5 grams) ground cinnamon
- 1/4 teaspoon (1 gram) ground nutmeg
- 1/4 teaspoon (1 gram) ground ginger
- 4 tablespoons (60 millilitres) water

Directions:

1. Preheat your oven to 180°C (350°F).
2. In a small bowl, combine the maple syrup, cinnamon, nutmeg, and ginger.
3. Place the pear halves, cut side up, in a baking dish. Drizzle the maple syrup mixture over the pears.
4. Pour the water into the bottom of the baking dish.
5. Cover the dish with aluminum foil and bake for 20 to 25 minutes, or until the pears are tender when pierced with a fork.
6. Remove from the oven and let cool for a few minutes before serving. You can serve them warm or at room temperature.

Nutritional Information: Per serving: 110 calories, 0.5g protein, 29g carbohydrates, 0.2g fat, 5g fiber, 0mg cholesterol, 2mg sodium, 210mg potassium.

Lemon and Blueberry Muffins

Yield: 6 servings | Prep time: 15 minutes | Cook time: 25 minutes

Ingredients:

- 200 grams plain flour
- 1 teaspoon (5 grams) baking powder
- 1/2 teaspoon (3 grams) baking soda
- 1/4 teaspoon (2 grams) salt
- 100 grams caster sugar
- 80 millilitres vegetable oil
- 2 large eggs
- Zest and juice of 1 lemon
- 150 grams fresh or frozen blueberries

Directions:

1. Preheat your oven to 180°C (350°F). Line a muffin tin with paper or silicone muffin cups.
2. In a large mixing bowl, whisk together the flour, baking powder, baking soda, and salt.
3. In a separate bowl, beat the sugar and oil together until well combined. Add the eggs one at a time, beating well after each addition. Stir in the lemon zest and juice.
4. Gradually add the wet ingredients to the dry ingredients, stirring until just combined. Do not overmix.
5. Gently fold in the blueberries.
6. Divide the batter evenly among the muffin cups. Bake for 20 to 25 minutes, or until a toothpick inserted into the centre of a muffin comes out clean.
7. Remove from the oven and let cool for 5 minutes in the tin before transferring to a wire rack to cool completely.

Nutritional Information: Per serving: 240 calories, 4g protein, 36g carbohydrates, 9g fat, 1g fiber, 55mg cholesterol, 210mg sodium, 75mg potassium.

Strawberry Shortcake

Yield: 6 servings | Prep time: 15 minutes | Cook time: 15 minutes

Ingredients:

- 250 grams strawberries, hulled and sliced
- 1 tablespoon (15 grams) granulated sugar
- 200 grams self-raising flour
- 1/2 teaspoon (2 grams) baking powder
- 60 grams unsalted butter, cold and diced
- 3 tablespoons (45 millilitres) milk
- 1 large egg, beaten
- 120 millilitres low-fat whipped cream (or non-dairy alternative)

Directions:

1. In a medium bowl, combine the sliced strawberries and sugar. Mix gently, cover, and refrigerate for 1 hour.
2. Preheat the oven to 220°C (425°F). Line a baking sheet with parchment paper.
3. In a large bowl, mix the flour and baking powder. Add the cold, diced butter and rub it into the flour using your fingertips until the mixture resembles coarse breadcrumbs.
4. Gradually add the milk and beaten egg to the flour mixture, stirring until a soft dough forms.
5. Drop spoonfuls of dough onto the prepared baking sheet, creating 6 shortcakes. Bake for 10-12 minutes or until golden brown.
6. Once baked, remove the shortcakes from the oven and let them cool on a wire rack.
7. To serve, slice each shortcake in half, spoon the strawberries onto the bottom half, top with whipped cream, and place the other half of the shortcake on top.

Nutritional Information: Per serving: 230 calories, 5g protein, 35g carbohydrates, 8g fat, 2g fiber, 45mg cholesterol, 190mg sodium, 150mg potassium.

Apple Crumble with Oat Topping

Yield: 6 servings | Prep time: 15 minutes | Cook time: 40 minutes

Ingredients:

- 4 medium-sized apples (approximately 500 grams), peeled, cored, and sliced
- 1 tablespoon (15 grams) granulated sugar
- 1 teaspoon (5 millilitres) lemon juice
- 1 teaspoon (5 grams) ground cinnamon
- 75 grams rolled oats
- 50 grams plain flour
- 50 grams unsalted butter, cold and diced
- 2 tablespoons (30 grams) brown sugar

Directions:

1. Preheat the oven to 180°C (350°F).
2. In a medium-sized mixing bowl, combine the sliced apples, granulated sugar, lemon juice, and cinnamon. Stir until the apples are evenly coated with the sugar and cinnamon.
3. Transfer the apple mixture to a baking dish, spreading it out in an even layer.
4. In another medium-sized mixing bowl, combine the rolled oats, plain flour, and cold, diced butter. Rub the butter into the flour and oats with your fingertips until the mixture resembles coarse crumbs.
5. Stir in the brown sugar, then sprinkle the oat mixture evenly over the apples in the baking dish.
6. Bake for 35-40 minutes or until the topping is golden brown and the apples are tender.
7. Remove from the oven and let cool slightly before serving.

Nutritional Information: Per serving: 190 calories, 2g protein, 32g carbohydrates, 7g fat, 4g fiber, 20mg cholesterol, 5mg sodium, 150mg potassium.

Almond and Raspberry Cake

Yield: 6 servings | Prep time: 15 minutes | Cook time: 35 minutes

Ingredients:

- 120 grams ground almonds
- 60 grams all-purpose flour
- 1 teaspoon (4 grams) baking powder
- 120 grams unsalted butter, at room temperature
- 60 grams granulated sugar
- 2 large eggs
- 1 teaspoon (5 millilitres) almond extract
- 150 grams fresh raspberries

Directions:

1. Preheat the oven to 180°C (350°F). Grease and line an 18 cm (7-inch) round cake tin with parchment paper.
2. In a medium-sized mixing bowl, combine the ground almonds, flour, and baking powder. Stir to mix well.
3. In a separate large mixing bowl, beat the butter and sugar together until light and creamy. Add the eggs one at a time, beating well after each addition. Stir in the almond extract.
4. Gradually fold the dry ingredients into the wet ingredients until just combined.
5. Gently fold in half of the raspberries, taking care not to crush them.
6. Transfer the batter to the prepared cake tin and level the surface. Scatter the remaining raspberries over the top of the cake.
7. Bake for 30-35 minutes or until a toothpick inserted into the centre of the cake comes out clean.
8. Allow the cake to cool in the tin for 10 minutes, then transfer it to a wire rack to cool completely.

Nutritional Information: Per serving: 285 calories, 6g protein, 20g carbohydrates, 21g fat, 3g fiber, 85mg cholesterol, 45mg sodium, 105mg potassium.

Mango and Lime Sorbet

Yield: 4 servings | Prep time: 15 minutes | Cook time: 0 minutes (Freeze time: 4 hours)

Ingredients:

- 400 grams ripe mangoes, peeled, pitted and chopped
- 80 millilitres (1/3 cup) fresh lime juice
- 80 grams granulated sugar
- 120 millilitres (1/2 cup) water

Directions:

1. In a small saucepan over medium heat, combine the sugar and water. Cook, stirring, until the sugar has dissolved. Remove from heat and allow to cool.
2. In a blender, combine the chopped mangoes and lime juice. Blend until smooth.
3. Gradually add the cooled sugar syrup to the mango mixture while continuing to blend. Blend until well combined.
4. Pour the mixture into a shallow, freezer-safe container and spread it out evenly.
5. Cover the container with a lid or plastic wrap and freeze for at least 4 hours or until the sorbet is firm.
6. Before serving, let the sorbet sit at room temperature for a few minutes to soften slightly. Scoop into serving bowls and enjoy.

Nutritional Information: Per serving: 115 calories, 0.5g protein, 30g carbohydrates, 0.3g fat, 1g fiber, 0mg cholesterol, 2mg sodium, 142mg potassium.

Lemon and Poppy Seed Scones

Yield: 6 servings | Prep time: 15 minutes | Cook time: 12 minutes

Ingredients:

- 225 grams self-raising flour
- 1/2 teaspoon baking powder
- 50 grams unsalted butter, chilled and cubed
- 25 grams granulated sugar
- 1 tablespoon poppy seeds
- Zest of 1 lemon
- 150 millilitres milk
- 1 tablespoon lemon juice
- 1 tablespoon milk (for glazing)

Directions:

1. Preheat your oven to 220°C (200°C fan-forced). Line a baking tray with parchment paper.
2. In a large bowl, sift together the flour and baking powder. Add the chilled butter and rub it into the flour with your fingertips until the mixture resembles fine breadcrumbs.
3. Stir in the sugar, poppy seeds, and lemon zest.
4. Gradually add the milk and lemon juice, stirring gently with a fork until a soft dough forms. Do not overmix.
5. Turn the dough out onto a floured surface and gently knead it a few times until it comes together. Pat or roll the dough out to a thickness of about 2 cm.
6. Use a round cutter (about 5 cm in diameter) to cut out the scones. Place them onto the prepared baking tray.
7. Brush the tops of the scones with the additional tablespoon of milk.
8. Bake for 10-12 minutes, or until the scones have risen and are golden brown on top.
9. Remove from the oven and allow to cool slightly before serving.

Nutritional Information: Per serving: 175 calories, 4g protein, 30g carbohydrates, 5g fat, 1g fiber, 14mg cholesterol, 102mg sodium, 92mg potassium.

Baked Peaches with Honey

Yield: 4 servings | Prep time: 5 minutes | Cook time: 25 minutes

Ingredients:

- 4 ripe peaches, halved and pitted
- 4 tablespoons honey
- 1/2 teaspoon ground cinnamon

Directions:

1. Preheat your oven to 180°C (160°C fan-forced).
2. Place the peach halves, cut-side up, in a baking dish.
3. Drizzle each peach half with 1/2 tablespoon of honey.
4. Sprinkle a pinch of cinnamon over each peach.
5. Cover the baking dish with foil and bake in the preheated oven for 20-25 minutes, or until the peaches are tender.
6. Remove from the oven and let cool for a few minutes before serving. Drizzle the peaches with any remaining juices in the baking dish.

Nutritional Information: Per serving: 76 calories, 0.6g protein, 19.6g carbohydrates, 0.2g fat, 1.4g fiber, 0mg cholesterol, 0mg sodium, 181mg potassium.

Rice Pudding with Raisins

Yield: 4 servings | Prep time: 5 minutes | Cook time: 35 minutes

Ingredients:

- 100g arborio rice
- 800ml unsweetened almond milk
- 50g raisins
- 2 tablespoons honey
- 1 teaspoon vanilla extract
- 1/4 teaspoon ground cinnamon

Directions:

1. In a medium saucepan, bring the almond milk to a simmer over medium heat. Add the rice and reduce the heat to low.
2. Cook, stirring occasionally, for 25-30 minutes, or until the rice is tender and the mixture has thickened.
3. Remove from heat and stir in the raisins, honey, vanilla extract, and cinnamon.
4. Divide the rice pudding into four serving bowls and allow it to cool slightly before serving.

Nutritional Information: Per serving: 188 calories, 2.3g protein, 38.5g carbohydrates, 2.3g fat, 1.7g fiber, 0mg cholesterol, 80mg sodium, 86mg potassium.

Vanilla Panna Cotta with Berries

Yield: 4 servings | Prep time: 10 minutes | Cook time: 5 minutes (plus at least 4 hours of refrigeration)

Ingredients:

- 300ml unsweetened almond milk
- 1 vanilla pod, split lengthwise, seeds scraped
- 1 tablespoon honey
- 7g unflavored gelatin powder
- 150g mixed berries (strawberries, raspberries, and blueberries)

Directions:

1. In a small bowl, sprinkle the gelatin over 50ml of the almond milk. Let it sit for 5 minutes to allow the gelatin to soften.
2. In a saucepan, heat the remaining 250ml of almond milk over medium heat. Add the vanilla pod and seeds, and honey. Heat until hot, but not boiling.
3. Remove the saucepan from the heat and add the gelatin mixture. Stir until the gelatin has completely dissolved.
4. Divide the mixture among four ramekins or dessert molds. Cover with plastic wrap and refrigerate for at least 4 hours or until set.
5. To serve, run a knife around the edge of each panna cotta to loosen it from the mold. Invert each one onto a serving plate. Top with the mixed berries.

Nutritional Information: Per serving: 55 calories, 1.8g protein, 10.5g carbohydrates, 1g fat, 1.2g fiber, 0mg cholesterol, 16mg sodium, 60mg potassium.

Coconut and Pineapple Cake

Yield: 6 servings | Prep time: 15 minutes | Cook time: 30 minutes

Ingredients:

- 200g pineapple, finely chopped
- 50g desiccated coconut
- 150g all-purpose flour
- 75g sugar
- 1 teaspoon baking powder
- 1/2 teaspoon baking soda
- 1/4 teaspoon salt
- 60ml coconut oil, melted
- 2 large eggs
- 1 teaspoon vanilla extract
- 100ml almond milk

Directions:

1. Preheat the oven to 180°C (350°F). Grease a 20cm (8-inch) round cake pan and line with parchment paper.
2. In a large bowl, whisk together the flour, sugar, baking powder, baking soda, and salt.
3. In another bowl, whisk together the coconut oil, eggs, vanilla extract, and almond milk.
4. Add the wet ingredients to the dry ingredients and mix until just combined.
5. Fold in the chopped pineapple and desiccated coconut.
6. Pour the batter into the prepared cake pan and smooth the top.
7. Bake for 30 minutes or until a toothpick inserted into the center comes out clean.
8. Allow the cake to cool in the pan for 10 minutes, then remove from the pan and allow to cool completely on a wire rack.

Nutritional Information: Per serving: 276 calories, 5g protein, 35g carbohydrates, 13g fat, 2g fiber, 62mg cholesterol, 238mg sodium, 135mg potassium.

Raspberry and Almond Tart

Yield: 6 servings | Prep time: 20 minutes | Cook time: 35 minutes

Ingredients:

- 150g all-purpose flour
- 75g unsalted butter, cold and cubed
- 2 tablespoons cold water
- 100g ground almonds
- 75g sugar
- 1 large egg
- 1/2 teaspoon vanilla extract
- 200g fresh raspberries
- 1 tablespoon icing sugar, for dusting

Directions:

1. In a food processor, combine the flour and butter until the mixture resembles coarse crumbs. Add the cold water and process until a dough forms. Wrap the dough in plastic wrap and refrigerate for 30 minutes.
2. Preheat the oven to 190°C (375°F). Roll out the dough on a lightly floured surface and fit it into a 23cm (9-inch) tart pan. Trim any excess dough and prick the bottom with a fork.
3. In a medium bowl, mix together the ground almonds, sugar, egg, and vanilla extract until well combined. Spread the almond mixture over the tart shell.
4. Arrange the raspberries on top of the almond mixture.
5. Bake for 30-35 minutes, or until the tart is golden brown and the filling is set.
6. Allow the tart to cool in the pan before removing it. Dust with icing sugar before serving.

Nutritional Information: Per serving: 280 calories, 6g protein, 34g carbohydrates, 15g fat, 4g fiber, 57mg cholesterol, 70mg sodium, 125mg potassium.

Chocolate and Almond Biscotti

Yield: 6 servings | Prep time: 15 minutes | Cook time: 35 minutes

Ingredients:

- 150g all-purpose flour
- 50g cocoa powder
- 1 teaspoon baking powder
- 1/4 teaspoon salt
- 75g sugar
- 2 large eggs
- 1 teaspoon vanilla extract
- 50g almonds, roughly chopped
- 50g dark chocolate chips

Directions:

1. Preheat the oven to 180°C (350°F). Line a baking sheet with parchment paper.
2. In a large bowl, whisk together the flour, cocoa powder, baking powder, and salt.
3. In another bowl, beat the eggs, sugar, and vanilla extract until well combined.
4. Gradually add the dry ingredients to the wet ingredients, mixing until just combined.
5. Stir in the chopped almonds and chocolate chips.
6. Transfer the dough onto the prepared baking sheet and shape into a log approximately 30cm (12 inches) long and 5cm (2 inches) wide.
7. Bake for 25 minutes, then remove from the oven and allow to cool for 10 minutes.
8. Cut the log into 1.5cm (0.5 inch) wide slices and arrange them on the baking sheet.
9. Return to the oven and bake for an additional 10 minutes, turning the biscotti halfway through to ensure even baking.
10. Allow the biscotti to cool on the baking sheet before serving.

Nutritional Information: Per serving: 215 calories, 6g protein, 34g carbohydrates, 7g fat, 3g fiber, 62mg cholesterol, 185mg sodium, 135mg potassium.

Chocolate Mousse with Raspberries

Yield: 4 servings | Prep time: 15 minutes | Cook time: 0 minutes (chilling time: 2 hours)

Ingredients:

- 100g dark chocolate (70% cocoa), chopped
- 2 large egg yolks
- 30g granulated sugar
- 120ml whipped cream (dairy-free if needed)
- 1 teaspoon vanilla extract
- 100g fresh raspberries
- Mint leaves for garnish (optional)

Directions:

1. In a heatproof bowl, melt the dark chocolate over a pot of simmering water (double boiler) or in the microwave in 30-second intervals. Once melted, set aside to cool slightly.
2. In a medium bowl, whisk the egg yolks and sugar until thick and pale. Gradually whisk in the melted chocolate until well combined.
3. In a separate bowl, whip the cream until stiff peaks form. Gently fold the whipped cream into the chocolate mixture until fully combined.
4. Spoon the chocolate mousse into serving glasses or bowls. Cover with plastic wrap and refrigerate for at least 2 hours or until set.
5. Before serving, top each mousse with fresh raspberries and garnish with mint leaves if desired.

Nutritional Information: Per serving: 260 calories, 4g protein, 24g carbohydrates, 18g fat, 3g fiber, 105mg cholesterol, 30mg sodium, 150mg potassium.

Lemon and Raspberry Cheesecake

Yield: 6 servings | Prep time: 15 minutes | Cook time: 40 minutes

Ingredients:

- 150g digestive biscuits, crushed
- 75g unsalted butter, melted
- 400g low-fat cream cheese
- 100g granulated sugar
- 2 large eggs
- Zest and juice of 2 lemons
- 150g fresh raspberries
- 2 tablespoons icing sugar, for dusting

Directions:

1. Preheat your oven to 180°C (350°F). Mix the crushed biscuits and melted butter together in a bowl, then press into the bottom of a 23cm (9-inch) springform tin. Bake for 10 minutes, then remove from the oven and set aside.
2. In a large bowl, beat the cream cheese until smooth. Add the sugar and beat until combined. Beat in the eggs one at a time, then stir in the lemon zest and juice.
3. Pour the cream cheese mixture over the biscuit base. Scatter the raspberries over the top.
4. Bake for 30 minutes, or until the cheesecake is set but still slightly wobbly in the center. Turn off the oven, crack the door open, and let the cheesecake cool for 1 hour. Then remove from the oven and cool completely.
5. Refrigerate the cheesecake for at least 4 hours, or overnight, before serving. Dust with icing sugar before serving.

Nutritional Information: Per serving: 280 calories, 6g protein, 34g carbohydrates, 15g fat, 2g fiber, 75mg cholesterol, 230mg sodium, 125mg potassium.

Blueberry and Lemon Bread

Yield: 6 servings | Prep time: 15 minutes | Cook time: 50 minutes

Ingredients:

- 190g plain flour
- 1/2 teaspoon baking soda
- 1 teaspoon baking powder
- 1/4 teaspoon salt
- 80g unsalted butter, softened
- 150g granulated sugar
- 2 large eggs
- Zest and juice of 2 lemons
- 120ml low-fat milk
- 150g fresh blueberries

Directions:

1. Preheat your oven to 180°C (350°F). Grease and line a 23cm x 13cm (9-inch x 5-inch) loaf tin with parchment paper.
2. In a medium bowl, whisk together the flour, baking soda, baking powder, and salt. Set aside.
3. In a large bowl, beat the butter and sugar together until light and fluffy. Beat in the eggs one at a time, then stir in the lemon zest and juice.
4. Add the dry ingredients to the wet ingredients in three batches, alternating with the milk. Stir until just combined.
5. Gently fold in the blueberries, then pour the batter into the prepared loaf tin.
6. Bake for 50 minutes, or until a toothpick inserted into the center comes out clean. Allow the bread to cool in the tin for 10 minutes, then transfer to a wire rack to cool completely.

Nutritional Information: Per serving: 280 calories, 5g protein, 45g carbohydrates, 10g fat, 2g fiber, 70mg cholesterol, 220mg sodium, 110mg potassium.

Strawberry and Rhubarb Crumble

Yield: 6 servings | Prep time: 15 minutes | Cook time: 35 minutes

Ingredients:

Filling:

- 300g strawberries, hulled and halved
- 300g rhubarb, trimmed and cut into 2cm pieces
- 100g granulated sugar
- 2 tablespoons cornstarch
- 1 teaspoon vanilla extract

Crumble Topping:

- 150g plain flour
- 75g rolled oats
- 100g brown sugar
- 1/2 teaspoon cinnamon
- 100g unsalted butter, cold and cut into small cubes

Directions:

1. Preheat your oven to 190°C (375°F). Grease a 20cm x 20cm (8-inch x 8-inch) baking dish.
2. In a large mixing bowl, combine the strawberries, rhubarb, sugar, cornstarch, and vanilla extract. Mix well, then pour the mixture into the prepared baking dish.
3. In a separate bowl, mix the flour, rolled oats, brown sugar, and cinnamon together. Add the cold butter and use your fingers to rub it into the dry ingredients until the mixture resembles coarse crumbs.
4. Sprinkle the crumble topping evenly over the fruit filling in the baking dish.
5. Bake for 35 minutes, or until the crumble is golden brown and the filling is bubbly. Let the crumble cool for at least 10 minutes before serving.

Nutritional Information: Per serving: 350 calories, 4g protein, 60g carbohydrates, 12g fat, 3g fiber, 35mg cholesterol, 10mg sodium, 250mg potassium.

Carrot and Walnut Cake

Yield: 8 servings | Prep time: 20 minutes | Cook time: 35 minutes

Ingredients:

- 200g grated carrots
- 150g all-purpose flour
- 75g chopped walnuts
- 150g granulated sugar
- 60ml vegetable oil
- 2 large eggs
- 1 teaspoon baking powder
- 1/2 teaspoon baking soda
- 1/2 teaspoon ground cinnamon
- 1/4 teaspoon ground nutmeg
- 1/4 teaspoon salt
- 1 teaspoon vanilla extract

For the frosting (optional):

- 100g cream cheese, softened
- 30g powdered sugar
- 1/2 teaspoon vanilla extract

Directions:

1. Preheat your oven to 180°C (160°C fan-forced) and grease an 8-inch round cake tin with oil or butter.
2. In a large bowl, whisk together the eggs, oil, sugar, and vanilla extract until well combined. Add the grated carrots and mix until incorporated.
3. In a separate bowl, sift together the flour, baking powder, baking soda, cinnamon, nutmeg, and salt. Gradually fold the dry ingredients into the wet mixture until just combined. Stir in the chopped walnuts.
4. Pour the batter into the prepared cake tin and smooth the top with a spatula. Bake for 35-40 minutes or until a toothpick inserted into the center comes out clean.
5. Allow the cake to cool in the tin for 10 minutes, then transfer it to a wire rack to cool completely.
6. If using the frosting, mix together the cream cheese, powdered sugar, and vanilla extract until smooth. Spread the frosting on top of the cooled cake, slice, and serve.

Nutritional Information: Per serving (without frosting): 295 calories, 5g protein, 36g carbohydrates, 15g fat, 2g fiber, 53mg cholesterol, 220mg sodium, 150mg potassium.

Peach and Almond Tart

Yield: 6 servings | Prep time: 20 minutes | Cook time: 45 minutes

Ingredients:

- 175g all-purpose flour
- 85g cold unsalted butter, cubed
- 30g granulated sugar
- 1 large egg yolk
- 1-2 tablespoons cold water
- 4 ripe peaches, pitted and sliced
- 60g ground almonds
- 60g granulated sugar
- 1 large egg
- 1/2 teaspoon almond extract
- 1/4 teaspoon vanilla extract
- 1 tablespoon flaked almonds (optional)
- Powdered sugar, for dusting (optional)

Directions:

1. In a large bowl, combine the flour and sugar. Add the cubed butter and use a pastry cutter or your fingers to work it into the flour until the mixture resembles coarse crumbs. Add the egg yolk and 1 tablespoon of cold water, mixing until the dough comes together. Add additional water if needed. Shape the dough into a disk, wrap it in plastic wrap, and refrigerate for 15 minutes.
2. Preheat your oven to 180°C (160°C fan-forced). Roll out the chilled dough on a lightly floured surface and fit it into a 9-inch tart pan, trimming any excess. Prick the bottom of the crust with a fork and refrigerate for another 10 minutes.
3. In a medium bowl, combine the ground almonds, sugar, egg, almond extract, and vanilla extract. Mix until smooth. Spread the almond mixture evenly over the tart crust. Arrange the peach slices on top of the almond filling.
4. Bake the tart in the preheated oven for 45 minutes, or until the filling is set and the crust is golden brown. Sprinkle flaked almonds on top during the last 5 minutes of baking, if desired.
5. Allow the tart to cool in the pan on a wire rack. Dust with powdered sugar before serving, if desired.

Nutritional Information: Per serving: 335 calories, 6g protein, 45g carbohydrates, 15g fat, 3g fiber, 80mg cholesterol, 80mg sodium, 220mg potassium.

Beverages and Drinks

Lemon and Cucumber Detox Water

Yield: 6 servings | Prep time: 10 minutes | Cook time: 0 minutes

Ingredients:

- 1.5 litres of water
- 1 medium lemon, thinly sliced
- 1 medium cucumber, thinly sliced
- Fresh mint leaves (optional)
- Ice cubes (optional)

Directions:

1. In a large pitcher, combine the water, lemon slices, and cucumber slices. If desired, add a handful of fresh mint leaves for extra flavour.
2. Cover the pitcher and refrigerate for at least 2 hours to allow the flavours to infuse. For best results, refrigerate overnight.
3. Serve the detox water chilled, over ice if desired. You can also strain out the cucumber and lemon slices before serving, or leave them in for added visual appeal and flavour.

Nutritional Information: Per serving: 5 calories, 0g protein, 1g carbohydrates, 0g fat, 0g fiber, 0mg cholesterol, 10mg sodium, 70mg potassium.

Cranberry and Orange Iced Tea

Yield: 6 servings | Prep time: 10 minutes | Cook time: 10 minutes

Ingredients:

- 1.5 litres of water
- 4 black tea bags
- 100ml cranberry juice (unsweetened)
- 1 medium orange, thinly sliced
- Fresh mint leaves (optional)
- Ice cubes
- Sweetener of choice (optional)

Directions:

1. In a large pot, bring 1.5 litres of water to a boil. Once boiling, remove from heat and add the black tea bags. Allow the tea to steep for 5 minutes, then remove the tea bags.
2. Add the cranberry juice to the pot and stir to combine. Allow the tea to cool to room temperature.
3. Once cooled, pour the tea into a large pitcher. Add the orange slices and fresh mint leaves, if desired.
4. Refrigerate the tea for at least 2 hours to chill. Serve over ice, and sweeten with your choice of sweetener if desired.

Nutritional Information: Per serving: 15 calories, 0g protein, 4g carbohydrates, 0g fat, 0g fiber, 0mg cholesterol, 5mg sodium, 40mg potassium.

Apple and Ginger Smoothie

Yield: 2 servings | Prep time: 10 minutes | Cook time: 0 minutes

Ingredients:

- 2 medium apples, cored and chopped
- 2.5 cm fresh ginger root, peeled and grated
- 240 ml water
- 1 teaspoon honey (optional)
- Ice cubes (optional)

Directions:

1. In a blender, combine the chopped apples, grated ginger, and water.
2. Blend until smooth. If the smoothie is too thick, you can add more water as needed.
3. If desired, add honey to sweeten the smoothie to your taste.
4. Pour the smoothie into two glasses. Add ice cubes if desired, and serve immediately.

Nutritional Information: Per serving: 52 calories, 0.3g protein, 14g carbohydrates, 0.2g fat, 2.5g fiber, 0mg cholesterol, 1mg sodium, 107mg potassium.

Strawberry and Basil Lemonade

Yield: 4 servings | Prep time: 10 minutes | Cook time: 0 minutes

Ingredients:

- 500g strawberries, hulled and halved
- 10 fresh basil leaves
- 2 lemons, juiced
- 1 liter water
- 4 teaspoons sugar substitute (or to taste)

Directions:

1. In a blender, combine the strawberries, basil leaves, and lemon juice. Blend until smooth.
2. Strain the mixture through a fine-mesh sieve into a large pitcher, discarding the solids.
3. Add the water and sugar substitute to the pitcher. Stir well to combine.
4. Taste and adjust the sweetness if needed.
5. Serve chilled over ice, garnished with additional basil leaves and strawberry slices if desired.

Nutritional Information: Per serving: 40 calories, 1g protein, 10g carbohydrates, 0.4g fat, 2.5g fiber, 0mg cholesterol, 5mg sodium, 170mg potassium.

Pineapple and Mint Infused Water

Yield: 4 servings | Prep time: 10 minutes | Cook time: 0 minutes

Ingredients:

- 500g fresh pineapple, cut into small chunks
- 10 fresh mint leaves
- 1 liter water
- Ice cubes (optional)

Directions:

1. In a large pitcher, combine the pineapple chunks and mint leaves.
2. Add the water to the pitcher and stir gently to combine.
3. Refrigerate for at least 2 hours, allowing the flavors to infuse. The longer it sits, the more flavorful the water will be.
4. Serve the infused water chilled, over ice if desired. Use a strainer to serve if you prefer to avoid the fruit pieces in your glass.
5. Garnish with additional mint leaves if desired.

Nutritional Information: Per serving: 30 calories, 0.4g protein, 8g carbohydrates, 0.1g fat, 1g fiber, 0mg cholesterol, 2mg sodium, 85mg potassium.

Raspberry and Lime Sparkling Water

Yield: 4 servings | Prep time: 5 minutes | Cook time: 0 minutes

Ingredients:

- 150g fresh raspberries
- 1 lime, juiced and zest grated
- 1 liter sparkling water
- Ice cubes (optional)
- Fresh mint leaves for garnish (optional)

Directions:

1. In a large pitcher, muddle the raspberries gently with a muddler or the back of a spoon.
2. Add the lime juice and zest to the pitcher.
3. Pour in the sparkling water and gently stir to combine.
4. Serve the sparkling water over ice, if desired. Garnish with fresh mint leaves for an extra touch of freshness.
5. Enjoy immediately as the sparkling water is best when served fresh.

Nutritional Information: Per serving: 15 calories, 0.4g protein, 4g carbohydrates, 0.1g fat, 1.2g fiber, 0mg cholesterol, 1mg sodium, 37mg potassium.

Mango and Coconut Smoothie

Yield: 4 servings | Prep time: 10 minutes | Cook time: 0 minutes

Ingredients:

- 2 ripe mangoes, peeled and pitted (approximately 400g)
- 400ml coconut milk (choose a low-fat version if possible)
- 2 tbsp honey or maple syrup (optional)
- Ice cubes (optional)

Directions:

1. In a blender, combine the mangoes, coconut milk, and honey or maple syrup if desired.
2. Blend until smooth and creamy.
3. If you prefer a colder smoothie, add ice cubes and blend again until the ice is crushed.
4. Pour the smoothie into glasses and serve immediately.

Nutritional Information: Per serving: 188 calories, 2g protein, 28g carbohydrates, 8g fat, 2g fiber, 0mg cholesterol, 13mg sodium, 280mg potassium.

Orange and Carrot Juice

Yield: 4 servings | Prep time: 10 minutes | Cook time: 0 minutes

Ingredients:

- 4 large oranges, peeled (approximately 600g)
- 2 large carrots, peeled and chopped (approximately 150g)
- 240ml water
- 1 tbsp honey or maple syrup (optional)
- Ice cubes (optional)

Directions:

1. In a blender or juicer, combine the oranges, carrots, and water.
2. Blend or juice until smooth. If using a blender, strain the juice through a fine-mesh sieve to remove any pulp.
3. If desired, add honey or maple syrup to sweeten the juice.
4. If you prefer a colder juice, add ice cubes and stir until chilled.
5. Pour the juice into glasses and serve immediately.

Nutritional Information: Per serving: 96 calories, 2g protein, 23g carbohydrates, 0.4g fat, 4g fiber, 0mg cholesterol, 38mg sodium, 421mg potassium.

Berry and Almond Milk Smoothie

Yield: 2 servings | Prep time: 5 minutes | Cook time: 0 minutes

Ingredients:

- 200g mixed berries (strawberries, blueberries, and raspberries)
- 240ml unsweetened almond milk
- 1 tbsp chia seeds (optional)
- 1 tbsp honey or maple syrup (optional)
- Ice cubes (optional)

Directions:

1. In a blender, combine the mixed berries, almond milk, chia seeds (if using), and honey or maple syrup (if using).
2. Blend until smooth. If you prefer a colder smoothie, add ice cubes and blend until chilled.
3. Pour the smoothie into glasses and serve immediately.
4. Optional: Garnish with a few berries and a sprinkle of chia seeds on top.

Nutritional Information: Per serving: 105 calories, 3g protein, 21g carbohydrates, 3g fat, 7g fiber, 0mg cholesterol, 93mg sodium, 115mg potassium.

Peach and Lemon Iced Tea

Yield: 6 servings | Prep time: 10 minutes | Cook time: 5 minutes

Ingredients:

- 4 black tea bags
- 1.5 litres boiling water
- 4 ripe peaches, sliced
- 1 lemon, sliced
- 2 tbsp honey or sugar (optional)
- Ice cubes

Directions:

1. Place the tea bags in a large pitcher or jug. Pour the boiling water over the tea bags and let them steep for 5 minutes.
2. Remove the tea bags and let the tea cool to room temperature.
3. Add the sliced peaches and lemon slices to the pitcher.
4. If you like your iced tea sweet, add the honey or sugar and stir until dissolved.
5. Chill the tea in the refrigerator for at least 1-2 hours.
6. Serve the iced tea over ice cubes and garnish with additional peach and lemon slices if desired.

Nutritional Information: Per serving: 30 calories, 1g protein, 8g carbohydrates, 0g fat, 1g fiber, 0mg cholesterol, 4mg sodium, 87mg potassium.

Cucumber and Lime Cooler

Yield: 6 servings | Prep time: 10 minutes | Cook time: 0 minutes

Ingredients:

- 1 large cucumber, sliced
- 2 limes, sliced
- 1.5 litres cold water
- 2 tbsp honey or sugar (optional)
- Ice cubes
- Fresh mint leaves for garnish (optional)

Directions:

1. In a large pitcher or jug, combine the cucumber and lime slices.
2. Add the cold water to the pitcher and stir to combine.
3. If you like your cooler sweet, add the honey or sugar and stir until dissolved.
4. Refrigerate the cooler for at least 1-2 hours to allow the flavours to infuse.
5. Serve the cooler over ice cubes and garnish with fresh mint leaves if desired.

Nutritional Information: Per serving: 20 calories, 0g protein, 6g carbohydrates, 0g fat, 1g fiber, 0mg cholesterol, 3mg sodium, 70mg potassium.

Cherry and Mint Iced Tea

Yield: 4 servings | Prep time: 10 minutes | Cook time: 10 minutes

Ingredients:

- 4 black tea bags
- 1 litre water
- 200g cherries, pitted and halved
- 20 fresh mint leaves
- 4 tbsp honey or sugar (optional)
- Ice cubes
- Fresh mint sprigs and cherries for garnish (optional)

Directions:

1. In a large saucepan, bring the water to a boil. Once boiling, remove from heat and add the tea bags. Allow the tea to steep for 5 minutes.
2. Remove the tea bags and add the honey or sugar, stirring until dissolved. Let the tea cool to room temperature.
3. In a large pitcher or jug, combine the tea, cherries, and mint leaves. Stir to combine.
4. Refrigerate the iced tea for at least 1-2 hours to allow the flavours to infuse.
5. Serve the iced tea over ice cubes and garnish with fresh mint sprigs and cherries if desired.

Nutritional Information: Per serving: 40 calories, 0g protein, 10g carbohydrates, 0g fat, 1g fiber, 0mg cholesterol, 4mg sodium, 60mg potassium.

Watermelon and Basil Lemonade

Yield: 4 servings | Prep time: 10 minutes | Cook time: 0 minutes

Ingredients:

- 500g watermelon, cubed and seeds removed
- 30g fresh basil leaves
- Juice of 2 lemons (approximately 60 ml)
- 1 litre cold water
- 2 tbsp honey or sugar (optional)
- Ice cubes
- Watermelon slices and basil leaves for garnish (optional)

Directions:

1. In a blender, combine the watermelon and basil leaves. Blend until smooth.
2. Strain the mixture through a fine-mesh sieve into a large pitcher or jug.
3. Add the lemon juice, cold water, and honey or sugar (if using). Stir to combine.
4. Refrigerate the lemonade for at least 1-2 hours to chill and allow the flavours to infuse.
5. Serve the lemonade over ice cubes and garnish with watermelon slices and basil leaves if desired.

Nutritional Information: Per serving: 40 calories, 0.5g protein, 10g carbohydrates, 0g fat, 0.5g fiber, 0mg cholesterol, 4mg sodium, 100mg potassium.

Kiwi and Strawberry Smoothie

Yield: 2 servings | Prep time: 10 minutes | Cook time: 0 minutes

Ingredients:

- 2 ripe kiwis, peeled and chopped
- 200g strawberries, hulled and chopped
- 240ml unsweetened almond milk
- 1 tbsp honey (optional)
- Ice cubes (optional)

Directions:

1. In a blender, combine the kiwis, strawberries, almond milk, and honey (if using). Blend until smooth.
2. If desired, add ice cubes and blend again until smooth and chilled.
3. Pour the smoothie into glasses and serve immediately.

Nutritional Information: Per serving: 85 calories, 1.5g protein, 20g carbohydrates, 1.5g fat, 4g fiber, 0mg cholesterol, 85mg sodium, 350mg potassium.

Apple and Cinnamon Infused Water

Yield: 4 servings | Prep time: 5 minutes | Cook time: 0 minutes

Ingredients:

- 1 large apple, thinly sliced
- 2 cinnamon sticks
- 1.5 liters of water
- Ice cubes (optional)

Directions:

1. In a large pitcher, add the apple slices and cinnamon sticks.
2. Pour the water over the apples and cinnamon sticks.
3. Refrigerate for at least 2 hours to allow the flavors to infuse into the water. For a stronger flavor, refrigerate overnight.
4. Serve chilled with ice cubes if desired.

Nutritional Information: Per serving: 15 calories, 0g protein, 4g carbohydrates, 0g fat, 1g fiber, 0mg cholesterol, 5mg sodium, 50mg potassium.

Blueberry and Lemon Sparkling Water

Yield: 4 servings | Prep time: 5 minutes | Cook time: 0 minutes

Ingredients:

- 100g fresh blueberries
- 1 lemon, thinly sliced
- 1 liter sparkling water
- Ice cubes (optional)

Directions:

1. In a large pitcher, add the blueberries and lemon slices.
2. Pour the sparkling water over the blueberries and lemon slices.
3. Refrigerate for at least 1 hour to allow the flavors to infuse into the water.
4. Serve chilled with ice cubes if desired.

Nutritional Information: Per serving: 10 calories, 0g protein, 3g carbohydrates, 0g fat, 1g fiber, 0mg cholesterol, 1mg sodium, 20mg potassium.

Blackberry and Mint Iced Tea

Yield: 4 servings | Prep time: 5 minutes | Cook time: 5 minutes

Ingredients:

- 4 tea bags of black tea (preferably caffeine-free)
- 800ml hot water
- 100g fresh blackberries
- 4 sprigs fresh mint
- Ice cubes
- Lemon slices (optional)
- Sweetener to taste (optional)

Directions:

1. In a large pitcher, steep the tea bags in hot water for 3-5 minutes. Remove the tea bags and let the tea cool.
2. Add the fresh blackberries and mint sprigs to the cooled tea.
3. Refrigerate for at least 1 hour to allow the flavors to infuse.
4. Serve the iced tea over ice cubes and garnish with lemon slices if desired.
5. Add sweetener to taste if needed.

Nutritional Information: Per serving: 15 calories, 0g protein, 4g carbohydrates, 0g fat, 2g fiber, 0mg cholesterol, 2mg sodium, 55mg potassium.

Pomegranate and Orange Sparkler

Yield: 4 servings | Prep time: 10 minutes | Cook time: 0 minutes

Ingredients:

- 240ml pomegranate juice
- 240ml orange juice
- 480ml sparkling water
- 4 orange slices, for garnish
- Ice cubes

Directions:

1. In a pitcher, combine the pomegranate juice and orange juice. Mix well.
2. Fill each glass with ice cubes.
3. Pour the juice mixture over the ice cubes, filling each glass half full.
4. Top up each glass with sparkling water.
5. Garnish each glass with an orange slice.
6. Serve immediately.

Nutritional Information: Per serving: 60 calories, 1g protein, 14g carbohydrates, 0g fat, 1g fiber, 0mg cholesterol, 15mg sodium, 220mg potassium.

Ginger and Lemon Hot Tea

Yield: 4 servings | Prep time: 5 minutes | Cook time: 10 minutes

Ingredients:

- 1 litre of water
- 2 thumb-sized pieces of ginger, peeled and sliced
- 1 lemon, juiced
- 2 teaspoons of honey (optional)
- 4 tea bags of black tea (preferably caffeine-free)

Directions:

1. Bring the water to a boil in a large saucepan. Once boiling, add the ginger slices and simmer for about 5 minutes.
2. Remove from heat and add the tea bags. Allow the tea to steep for about 3-5 minutes.
3. Remove the tea bags and strain the tea to remove the ginger slices.
4. Stir in the lemon juice and honey if using.
5. Serve hot in individual cups.

Nutritional Information: Per serving: 10 calories, 0g protein, 3g carbohydrates, 0g fat, 0g fiber, 0mg cholesterol, 2mg sodium, 10mg potassium.

Seasonal and Holiday Recipes

Turkey and Cranberry Stuffing

Yield: 6 servings | Prep time: 15 minutes | Cook time: 45 minutes

Ingredients:

- 400g ground turkey (lean, minced)
- 80g dried cranberries, unsweetened
- 100g wholemeal bread crumbs
- 1 small onion, chopped
- 1 celery stalk, chopped
- 2 cloves garlic, minced
- 2 tsp fresh sage, chopped
- 1 tsp fresh thyme, chopped
- 1 tsp fresh rosemary, chopped
- 1/2 tsp black pepper
- 240ml low-sodium chicken broth

Directions:

1. Preheat the oven to 180°C (350°F).
2. In a large nonstick frying pan, cook the ground turkey over medium heat until no longer pink. Drain any excess fat and transfer the turkey to a large mixing bowl.
3. Add the dried cranberries, wholemeal bread crumbs, chopped onion, celery, garlic, sage, thyme, rosemary, and black pepper to the mixing bowl with the turkey. Mix well.
4. Gradually pour the low-sodium chicken broth into the mixture, stirring until the stuffing is evenly moistened.
5. Transfer the stuffing to a baking dish and cover with aluminum foil.
6. Bake in the preheated oven for 35 minutes. Remove the foil and bake for an additional 10 minutes, until the top is golden brown.
7. Serve hot.

Nutritional Information: Per serving: 230 calories, 22g protein, 20g carbohydrates, 7g fat, 3g fiber, 50mg cholesterol, 120mg sodium, 290mg potassium.

Spiced Apple Cider

Yield: 4 servings | Prep time: 5 minutes | Cook time: 15 minutes

Ingredients:

- 1 litre unsweetened apple juice
- 1 orange, sliced
- 4 whole cloves
- 2 cinnamon sticks
- 1 star anise
- 1 pinch of nutmeg

Directions:

1. In a large saucepan, combine the apple juice, orange slices, cloves, cinnamon sticks, star anise, and nutmeg. Bring the mixture to a simmer over medium heat.
2. Reduce the heat to low and let the cider simmer for 15 minutes, allowing the spices to infuse the apple juice.
3. Using a fine-mesh strainer, strain the cider into mugs or heatproof glasses, removing the spices and orange slices.
4. Serve the spiced apple cider hot, and enjoy!

Nutritional Information: Per serving: 120 calories, 0.3g protein, 30g carbohydrates, 0.2g fat, 0.5g fiber, 0mg cholesterol, 10mg sodium, 250mg potassium.

Roasted Pumpkin Soup

Yield: 6 servings | Prep time: 15 minutes | Cook time: 45 minutes

Ingredients:

- 1.5 kg pumpkin, peeled, seeded, and cut into cubes
- 1 large onion, chopped
- 3 cloves garlic, minced
- 1 tbsp olive oil
- 1 tsp ground cumin
- 1/2 tsp ground nutmeg
- 1/4 tsp ground black pepper
- 1.5 L low-sodium vegetable broth
- 100ml single cream (optional)

Directions:

1. Preheat your oven to 200°C (400°F). Place the pumpkin cubes on a baking sheet and drizzle with olive oil. Roast for about 25 minutes or until the pumpkin is tender and lightly browned. Remove from the oven and let it cool.
2. In a large saucepan, heat the remaining olive oil over medium heat. Add the chopped onions and cook until translucent, about 5 minutes.
3. Add the minced garlic, cumin, nutmeg, and black pepper. Cook for another 2 minutes, stirring frequently.
4. Add the roasted pumpkin to the saucepan and pour in the low-sodium vegetable broth. Bring the mixture to a boil, then reduce the heat and simmer for 15 minutes.
5. Using a hand blender or a countertop blender, puree the soup until smooth. If using a countertop blender, let the soup cool slightly before blending, and blend in batches.
6. Return the soup to the saucepan and heat over low heat until warmed through. Stir in the cream if desired, and adjust the seasoning as needed.
7. Serve hot.

Nutritional Information: Per serving: 100 calories, 2g protein, 23g carbohydrates, 2g fat, 5g fiber, 0mg cholesterol, 100mg sodium, 550mg potassium.

Roast Lamb with Rosemary and Garlic

Yield: 6 servings | Prep time: 10 minutes | Cook time: 120 minutes

Ingredients:

- 1 leg of lamb, about 2 kg
- 6 cloves of garlic, peeled and thinly sliced
- 2 tablespoons fresh rosemary, chopped
- 1 tablespoon olive oil
- 1 teaspoon salt
- 1/2 teaspoon black pepper

Directions:

1. Preheat your oven to 190°C (375°F).
2. Make small cuts all over the surface of the leg of lamb using a sharp knife. Insert slices of garlic into each cut.
3. In a small bowl, combine the chopped rosemary, olive oil, salt, and pepper. Rub this mixture all over the surface of the leg of lamb.
4. Place the lamb on a rack in a roasting pan. Roast the lamb for approximately 2 hours, or until the internal temperature reaches 70°C (160°F) for medium doneness.
5. Remove the lamb from the oven and let it rest for 10 minutes before carving. Serve with your choice of vegetables or salad.

Nutritional Information: Per serving: 370 calories, 55g protein, 1g carbohydrates, 15g fat, 0.1g fiber, 145mg cholesterol, 500mg sodium, 450mg potassium.

Hot Cross Buns with Raisins

Yield: 6 servings | Prep time: 120 minutes (including dough rising time) | Cook time: 20 minutes

Ingredients:

- 450g plain flour, plus extra for dusting
- 50g caster sugar
- 10g instant yeast
- 10g salt
- 150ml warm milk
- 1 large egg, beaten
- 50g unsalted butter, melted
- 100g raisins
- 2 tsp mixed spice
- Olive oil, for greasing

For the cross:

- 50g plain flour
- 50ml water

Directions:

1. Mix the flour, sugar, yeast, mixed spice, and salt in a large bowl. Add the warm milk, melted butter, and egg. Mix until a sticky dough forms. Add the raisins and mix until incorporated.
2. On a floured surface, knead the dough for 10 minutes until it's smooth and elastic. Place in a greased bowl, cover with a damp cloth, and leave to rise in a warm place for 1 hour or until doubled in size.
3. Preheat your oven to 220°C (200°C fan-assisted). Divide the risen dough into 12 equal portions and shape them into buns. Place them on a baking tray, ensuring there's space between each. Cover and let rise again for 30 minutes.
4. For the cross, mix the flour and water to make a thick paste. Transfer to a piping bag and pipe a cross onto each bun.
5. Bake in the preheated oven for 20 minutes or until golden brown.

Nutritional Information: Per serving: 340 calories, 9g protein, 66g carbohydrates, 6g fat, 2g fiber, 35mg cholesterol, 410mg sodium, 260mg potassium.

Grilled Sea Bass with Lemon Herb Sauce

Yield: 4 servings | Prep time: 10 minutes | Cook time: 12 minutes

Ingredients:

- 4 sea bass fillets, each weighing about 150g
- 2 tbsp olive oil
- Salt and pepper, to taste

For the lemon herb sauce:

- 3 tbsp olive oil
- 2 tbsp fresh lemon juice
- 1 tbsp chopped fresh parsley
- 1 tbsp chopped fresh basil
- 1 tbsp chopped fresh chives
- Salt and pepper, to taste

Directions:

1. Preheat the grill to medium-high heat. Drizzle the sea bass fillets with olive oil and season with salt and pepper.
2. Grill the fillets, skin side down, for about 5-6 minutes, until the skin is crispy. Flip the fillets and grill for an additional 2-3 minutes, until the fish flakes easily with a fork.
3. In a small bowl, whisk together the olive oil, lemon juice, parsley, basil, and chives for the sauce. Season with salt and pepper.
4. Remove the fillets from the grill and place them on serving plates. Spoon the lemon herb sauce over the top of each fillet and serve.

Nutritional Information: Per serving: 240 calories, 24g protein, 2g carbohydrates, 16g fat, 0g fiber, 60mg cholesterol, 70mg sodium, 410mg potassium.

Gingerbread Cookies with Lemon Icing

Yield: 6 servings | Prep time: 15 minutes | Cook time: 10 minutes

Ingredients:

- 150g plain flour
- 1/2 tsp baking soda
- 1/2 tsp ground ginger
- 1/2 tsp ground cinnamon
- 40g unsalted butter, softened
- 50g dark brown sugar
- 1 tbsp golden syrup
- 1 egg yolk

For the lemon icing:

- 100g icing sugar
- 1 tbsp lemon juice

Directions:

1. Preheat the oven to 180°C (160°C fan-assisted). Line a baking tray with parchment paper.
2. In a large bowl, combine the flour, baking soda, ginger, and cinnamon. In another bowl, cream together the butter, sugar, and golden syrup until light and fluffy. Add the egg yolk and mix until combined.
3. Gradually add the dry ingredients to the wet ingredients and mix until a dough forms. On a floured surface, roll out the dough to about 5mm thickness and cut into desired shapes.
4. Place the cut-out cookies on the prepared baking tray and bake for 10 minutes, or until golden brown. Allow the cookies to cool completely on a wire rack.
5. For the icing, combine the icing sugar and lemon juice until smooth. Drizzle the icing over the cooled cookies.

Nutritional Information: Per serving: 250 calories, 2g protein, 45g carbohydrates, 8g fat, 1g fiber, 35mg cholesterol, 120mg sodium, 40mg potassium.

Baked Ham with Pineapple Glaze

Yield: 6 servings | Prep time: 15 minutes | Cook time: 120 minutes

Ingredients:

- 2 kg boneless ham
- 1 small can (225 g) pineapple slices, juice reserved
- 1/2 teaspoon ground cloves
- 2 tablespoons brown sugar
- 1 tablespoon cornstarch
- 1 tablespoon Dijon mustard
- 1/2 teaspoon black pepper

Directions:

1. Preheat your oven to 160°C (325°F, gas mark 3). Place the ham in a large roasting pan, fat side up. Score the fat with a knife, creating a diamond pattern. Insert cloves into the scored fat.
2. In a saucepan, combine the reserved pineapple juice, brown sugar, cornstarch, mustard, and black pepper. Cook over medium heat, stirring constantly, until the mixture thickens and comes to a boil. Boil for 1 minute.
3. Brush the glaze over the ham. Bake in the preheated oven for 1 1/2 to 2 hours, or until the internal temperature reaches 71°C (160°F). Baste the ham with the glaze every 30 minutes during baking.
4. Arrange the pineapple slices on top of the ham during the last 30 minutes of baking.
5. Remove the ham from the oven and let it rest for 15 minutes before slicing. Serve the ham with the pineapple slices and any remaining glaze.

Nutritional Information: Per serving: 300 calories, 40g protein, 20g carbohydrates, 8g fat, 1g fiber, 90mg cholesterol, 1300mg sodium, 400mg potassium.

Easter Simnel Cake

Yield: 12 servings | Prep time: 25 minutes | Cook time: 140 minutes

Ingredients:

- 175g unsalted butter, softened
- 175g golden caster sugar
- 3 large eggs
- 250g self-raising flour
- 1 tsp baking powder
- 2 tsp mixed spice
- 250g mixed dried fruit (sultanas, currants, and raisins)
- Zest of 1 lemon
- 100g glace cherries, chopped
- 3 tbsp orange juice
- 500g marzipan

Directions:

1. Preheat your oven to 150°C (130°C fan). Grease and line an 18cm round, deep cake tin with baking parchment.
2. In a large mixing bowl, beat together the butter and sugar until light and fluffy. Gradually add the eggs, one at a time, mixing well after each addition.
3. Sift the flour, baking powder, and mixed spice into the bowl and fold in with a spatula until just combined. Stir in the dried fruit, lemon zest, cherries, and orange juice.
4. Roll out one-third of the marzipan to fit the base of the cake tin. Place it in the tin, then spoon half of the cake mixture on top. Roll out another third of the marzipan to fit the tin, place it on top of the cake mixture, then spoon the remaining mixture on top.
5. Bake the cake in the preheated oven for 2 hours and 20 minutes or until a skewer inserted into the center comes out clean. Remove from the oven and leave to cool in the tin.
6. When the cake is cool, remove from the tin and peel off the baking parchment. Roll out the remaining marzipan and place it on top of the cake. Create 11 small balls from the remaining marzipan and arrange them around the edge of the cake.

Nutritional Information: Per serving: 355 calories, 5g protein, 54g carbohydrates, 14g fat, 2g fiber, 65mg cholesterol, 105mg sodium, 145mg potassium.

Pimm's Cup with Fresh Fruit

Yield: 4 servings | Prep time: 10 minutes | Cook time: 0 minutes

Ingredients:

- 200ml Pimm's No. 1
- 600ml lemonade (low-sodium and sugar-free)
- 100g strawberries, hulled and sliced
- 1 small cucumber, thinly sliced
- 1 small orange, thinly sliced
- 4 sprigs of fresh mint
- Ice cubes

Directions:

1. In a large pitcher, combine the Pimm's No. 1 and lemonade.
2. Add the sliced strawberries, cucumber, and orange to the pitcher.
3. Gently muddle the fruit and cucumber with a long spoon to release some of their juices and flavors.
4. Add the sprigs of fresh mint and fill the pitcher with ice cubes.
5. Stir well to combine all the ingredients.
6. Serve the Pimm's Cup in individual glasses, making sure to include some of the fruit, cucumber, and mint in each serving.

Nutritional Information: Per serving: 150 calories, 1g protein, 28g carbohydrates, 0g fat, 1g fiber, 0mg cholesterol, 10mg sodium, 150mg potassium.

Summer Berry Trifle

Yield: 6 servings | Prep time: 30 minutes | Cook time: 0 minutes (no cooking required)

Ingredients:

- 150g sponge cake, cut into small cubes
- 200g strawberries, hulled and sliced
- 150g blueberries
- 150g raspberries
- 500g low-fat vanilla custard
- 250g low-fat Greek yogurt
- 2 tablespoons honey
- 1 teaspoon vanilla extract
- Fresh mint leaves for garnish

Directions:

1. In a large glass trifle dish or individual serving glasses, layer half of the sponge cake cubes at the bottom. Top with half of the strawberries, blueberries, and raspberries.
2. In a medium-sized bowl, mix together the low-fat vanilla custard, Greek yogurt, honey, and vanilla extract. Pour half of the custard mixture over the berries.
3. Repeat the layers with the remaining sponge cake cubes, berries, and custard mixture.
4. Refrigerate for at least 1 hour before serving to allow the flavors to meld.
5. Before serving, garnish with fresh mint leaves.

Nutritional Information: Per serving: 250 calories, 9g protein, 44g carbohydrates, 4g fat, 3g fiber, 15mg cholesterol, 150mg sodium, 300mg potassium.

Yorkshire Pudding with Gravy

Yield: 6 servings | Prep time: 10 minutes | Cook time: 25 minutes

Ingredients:

For the Yorkshire Pudding:

- 140g plain flour
- 4 large eggs
- 200ml low-fat milk
- 1/4 tsp salt
- 40ml vegetable oil

For the Gravy:

- 1 tbsp olive oil
- 1 small onion, finely chopped
- 2 tbsp plain flour
- 500ml low-sodium beef or vegetable broth
- Salt and pepper, to taste

Directions:

1. Preheat your oven to 220°C (425°F, gas mark 7). Pour a small amount of vegetable oil into each section of a 12-hole muffin tin or a large roasting tin, just enough to cover the bottom. Place the tin in the oven to heat up the oil.
2. In a mixing bowl, sift the flour and add the salt. Make a well in the center and crack the eggs into it. Gradually pour in the milk while whisking until you have a smooth batter. Let the batter rest for a few minutes.
3. Carefully remove the tin from the oven and pour the batter into the holes or roasting tin, filling them halfway. Place the tin back in the oven and bake for 20-25 minutes, or until the puddings have risen and are golden brown.
4. While the puddings are baking, make the gravy. In a saucepan, heat the olive oil over medium heat. Add the onion and cook until softened. Stir in the flour and cook for 2 minutes. Gradually add the broth while stirring, and bring to a simmer. Cook for 5 minutes, or until the gravy has thickened. Season with salt and pepper. Serve the Yorkshire puddings hot, with the gravy poured over the top.

Nutritional Information: Per serving: 220 calories, 8g protein, 23g carbohydrates, 11g fat, 1g fiber, 110mg cholesterol, 220mg sodium, 120mg potassium.

Grilled Sardines with Tomato Salsa

Yield: 4 servings | Prep time: 20 minutes | Cook time: 6 minutes

Ingredients:

- 8 fresh sardines, cleaned and gutted
- 1 tablespoon olive oil
- Salt and pepper to taste

For the Tomato Salsa:

- 4 ripe tomatoes, deseeded and finely chopped
- 1 small red onion, finely chopped
- 1 green chili, deseeded and finely chopped
- 1 tablespoon fresh coriander, chopped
- 1 tablespoon fresh lime juice
- Salt to taste

Directions:

1. Preheat the grill to medium-high heat.
2. In a medium bowl, combine the tomatoes, red onion, green chili, coriander, and lime juice. Season with salt, mix well, and set aside to let the flavors develop.
3. Rinse the sardines under cold water and pat dry with paper towels. Brush the sardines with olive oil and season with salt and pepper.
4. Grill the sardines for about 2-3 minutes on each side, or until they are cooked through and the skin is lightly charred.
5. Serve the grilled sardines on a plate and spoon the tomato salsa over the top.

Nutritional Information: Per serving: 180 calories, 21g protein, 6g carbohydrates, 8g fat, 2g fiber, 60mg cholesterol, 350mg sodium, 430mg potassium.

Strawberry and Cream Scones

Yield: 6 servings | Prep time: 20 minutes | Cook time: 12-15 minutes

Ingredients:

- 225g all-purpose flour
- 50g caster sugar
- 1 tablespoon baking powder
- 75g unsalted butter, cold and cubed
- 150g fresh strawberries, hulled and chopped
- 120ml double cream, plus extra for brushing
- 1 egg
- 1 teaspoon vanilla extract

Directions:

1. Preheat your oven to 220°C (200°C for fan ovens) and line a baking sheet with parchment paper.
2. In a large mixing bowl, whisk together the flour, sugar, and baking powder. Add the cold butter and use a pastry cutter or your fingertips to work the butter into the flour until the mixture resembles coarse crumbs.
3. Stir in the chopped strawberries.
4. In a separate bowl, whisk together the double cream, egg, and vanilla extract. Pour the wet ingredients into the dry ingredients and gently mix until a soft dough forms. Be careful not to overmix.
5. Turn the dough onto a floured surface and shape it into a circle, about 2.5 cm thick. Cut into 6 wedges.
6. Place the scones onto the prepared baking sheet, brush the tops with a little extra double cream, and bake for 12-15 minutes, or until the scones are golden brown on top.
7. Let the scones cool slightly before serving.

Nutritional Information: Per serving: 340 calories, 5g protein, 38g carbohydrates, 19g fat, 1g fiber, 70mg cholesterol, 150mg sodium, 90mg potassium.

Roasted Goose with Orange Sauce

Yield: 6 servings | Prep time: 20 minutes | Cook time: 180 minutes

Ingredients:

- 1 whole goose (about 4 kg), giblets removed and reserved
- Salt and pepper to taste (use salt sparingly for renal diet)
- 2 oranges, zested and juiced
- 1 large onion, quartered
- 3 cloves garlic, minced
- 2 tablespoons olive oil
- 250 ml low-sodium chicken broth
- 2 teaspoons cornflour
- 2 tablespoons water
- Fresh parsley, chopped, for garnish

Directions:

1. Preheat your oven to 180°C (350°F). Rinse the goose inside and out, then pat dry with paper towels. Season the goose with salt (sparingly) and pepper, both inside and out.
2. In a small bowl, mix together the orange zest, garlic, and olive oil. Rub this mixture all over the goose, including the cavity.
3. Stuff the cavity of the goose with the quartered onion. Truss the goose with kitchen twine and place it on a rack in a roasting pan.
4. Roast the goose in the preheated oven for about 3 hours, basting occasionally with the pan juices. The goose is done when the skin is browned and crispy, and the internal temperature reaches 75°C (165°F).
5. While the goose is roasting, prepare the orange sauce. In a small saucepan, combine the orange juice and chicken broth. Bring to a simmer and cook for about 10 minutes.
6. In a small bowl, mix together the cornflour and water to create a slurry. Gradually add this to the saucepan while stirring continuously. Continue cooking until the sauce thickens.
7. Once the goose is done, remove it from the oven and let it rest for about 10 minutes before carving.
8. Serve the roasted goose with the orange sauce and garnish with chopped parsley.

Nutritional Information: Per serving: 650 calories, 35g protein, 15g carbohydrates, 48g fat, 1g fiber, 180mg cholesterol, 350mg sodium, 450mg potassium.

Plum Pudding with Brandy Sauce

Yield: 6 servings | Prep time: 30 minutes | Cook time: 240 minutes

Ingredients:

For the Plum Pudding:

- 100g dried plums, chopped
- 75g raisins
- 50g currants
- 100g breadcrumbs
- 75g dark brown sugar
- 1/2 teaspoon ground cinnamon
- 1/4 teaspoon ground nutmeg
- 2 eggs, beaten
- 100g unsalted butter, melted
- 1 orange, zested and juiced
- 50g self-raising flour

For the Brandy Sauce:

- 250ml low-fat milk
- 25g caster sugar
- 1 tablespoon cornflour
- 2 tablespoons water
- 2 tablespoons brandy
- 1/2 teaspoon vanilla extract

Directions:

1. In a large mixing bowl, combine the dried plums, raisins, currants, breadcrumbs, brown sugar, cinnamon, and nutmeg. Stir well to combine.
2. In a separate bowl, whisk together the beaten eggs, melted butter, orange zest, and orange juice. Pour this wet mixture into the dry ingredients and stir until everything is well incorporated.
3. Gradually add the self-raising flour and mix until combined. Pour the batter into a greased and floured pudding basin, leaving about 2.5cm from the top for the pudding to rise.
4. Cover the basin with a piece of parchment paper and then a layer of aluminum foil, securing them with a string.
5. Steam the pudding in a large pot with a trivet or steamer insert, ensuring the water comes halfway up the sides of the pudding basin. Cover the pot and steam for 4 hours, adding more water as needed.
6. For the brandy sauce, in a small saucepan, heat the milk and caster sugar over medium heat until the sugar dissolves.
7. In a separate bowl, whisk together the cornflour and water to create a slurry. Gradually pour the slurry into the saucepan, stirring constantly until the sauce thickens.
8. Remove the sauce from heat and stir in the brandy and vanilla extract.
9. Once the plum pudding is ready, remove it from the pot and let it cool for a few minutes. Unmold the pudding onto a serving plate.
10. Serve the plum pudding warm, drizzled with the brandy sauce.

Nutritional Information: Per serving: 400 calories, 7g protein, 65g carbohydrates, 12g fat, 3g fiber, 80mg cholesterol, 200mg sodium, 400mg potassium.

Winter Vegetable Stew with Dumplings

Yield: 6 servings | Prep time: 15 minutes | Cook time: 45 minutes

Ingredients:

For the stew:

- 2 tbsp olive oil
- 1 large onion, chopped
- 2 cloves garlic, minced
- 2 large carrots, peeled and chopped
- 2 parsnips, peeled and chopped
- 1 small swede, peeled and chopped
- 1 leek, trimmed and chopped
- 1.5 litres low-sodium vegetable broth
- 2 bay leaves
- 1 tsp dried thyme
- Salt and pepper, to taste

For the dumplings:

- 125g plain flour
- 1 tsp baking powder
- 60g suet
- 5 tbsp cold water

Directions:

1. Heat the olive oil in a large pot over medium heat. Add the onions and cook until translucent, about 5 minutes. Add the garlic and cook for another 1 minute.
2. Add the carrots, parsnips, swede, and leek to the pot. Cook for another 5 minutes, stirring occasionally.
3. Pour in the vegetable broth and add the bay leaves, thyme, salt, and pepper. Bring to a boil, then reduce the heat and let it simmer for 20 minutes, or until the vegetables are tender.
4. While the stew is simmering, make the dumplings. In a mixing bowl, sift together the flour and baking powder. Add the suet and stir until well combined. Gradually add the water, stirring until the mixture comes together to form a dough.
5. Divide the dough into 12 small balls and drop them into the simmering stew. Cover the pot with a lid and let it cook for another 15 minutes, or until the dumplings are cooked through.
6. Remove the bay leaves from the stew and serve hot.

Nutritional Information: Per serving: 260 calories, 4g protein, 36g carbohydrates, 11g fat, 5g fiber, 10mg cholesterol, 320mg sodium, 350mg potassium.

Christmas Pudding with Custard

Yield: 6 servings | Prep time: 30 minutes | Cook time: 2 hours 30 minutes

Ingredients:

For the Christmas Pudding:

- 200g mixed dried fruit (sultanas, currants, raisins)
- 100ml apple juice
- 1 large apple, peeled and grated
- 50g self-raising flour
- 50g breadcrumbs
- 50g light brown sugar
- 1 tsp mixed spice
- 2 eggs
- 50g unsalted butter, melted
- For the Custard:
- 500ml whole milk
- 4 egg yolks
- 60g granulated sugar
- 1 tsp vanilla extract
- 1 tbsp cornstarch

Directions:

1. In a large bowl, combine the mixed dried fruit and apple juice. Let it soak for at least 1 hour or overnight if possible.
2. Preheat your oven to 160°C (320°F). In a separate bowl, combine the grated apple, self-raising flour, breadcrumbs, light brown sugar, and mixed spice. Add the soaked fruit, beaten eggs, and melted butter to the bowl. Mix everything until well combined.
3. Grease a 1-litre pudding basin. Pour the mixture into the basin and cover with a layer of baking paper and foil. Secure it with string or a rubber band.
4. Place the pudding basin into a large ovenproof dish. Fill the dish with water until it reaches halfway up the sides of the basin. Cover the dish with foil and bake in the oven for 2 hours and 30 minutes.
5. While the pudding is baking, prepare the custard. In a saucepan, heat the milk until it's almost boiling. In a separate bowl, whisk together the egg yolks, sugar, vanilla extract, and cornstarch until smooth.
6. Slowly pour the hot milk into the egg mixture, whisking constantly. Return the mixture to the saucepan and heat over low heat, stirring continuously until it thickens into a custard.
7. Once the pudding is done baking, remove it from the oven and let it cool slightly. Unmold the pudding onto a plate and serve it with the warm custard.

Nutritional Information: Per serving: 320 calories, 8g protein, 53g carbohydrates, 10g fat, 3g fiber, 150mg cholesterol, 150mg sodium, 300mg potassium.

Mince Pies with Orange Zest

Yield: 6 servings | Prep time: 20 minutes | Cook time: 20 minutes

Ingredients:

For the pastry:

- 200g plain flour
- 100g cold butter, cubed
- 50g icing sugar
- Zest of 1 orange
- 1 egg yolk
- 1-2 tbsp cold water

For the filling:

- 200g mincemeat
- Zest of 1 orange
- 1 tbsp orange juice

Directions:

1. Preheat the oven to 200°C (180°C fan, 400°F, gas mark 6).
2. In a large bowl, combine the plain flour and cold butter. Use your fingertips to rub the butter into the flour until the mixture resembles breadcrumbs. Stir in the icing sugar and orange zest.
3. Add the egg yolk and 1 tablespoon of cold water to the bowl. Mix everything together until it forms a dough. If the mixture is too dry, add a little more water until it comes together. Wrap the dough in cling film and chill in the fridge for 15 minutes.
4. Roll out the chilled dough on a floured surface until it's about 3mm thick. Use a round cookie cutter to cut out 12 circles of dough. Press the circles into a muffin tin, making sure they come up the sides to form a cup shape.
5. In a bowl, mix together the mincemeat, orange zest, and orange juice. Spoon the mixture into the pastry cups, filling them almost to the top.
6. Use the remaining dough to cut out 12 smaller circles or shapes for the pie tops. Place them on top of the mincemeat filling.
7. Bake in the preheated oven for 20 minutes, or until the pastry is golden and the filling is bubbling. Allow the pies to cool slightly in the tin before transferring them to a wire rack to cool completely.

Nutritional Information: Per serving: 300 calories, 4g protein, 40g carbohydrates, 15g fat, 2g fiber, 60mg cholesterol, 200mg sodium, 100mg potassium.

Printed in Great Britain
by Amazon

29855706R00053